Third Edition

ENGLISH For DAILY COMMUNICATION
Featuring American VS British English

Paul A. ETOGA

SOSEISHA

A Special Thanks

The authors and publisher are particularly grateful to the following people for their contribution to the development of ***ENGLISH FOR DAILY COMMUNICATION:***

Thanks to Mr. and Mrs. Arthur and Gertrude BOOTY, Mr. Bob AGAR for photographs taken in London, U.K.

To Mr. Henry OBAMA for photographs taken in Washington DC, and also for being my guide during my stay in Bethesda, MD, and my visits to D.C. as well as in my travels in the States of Maryland and Virginia.

To Mrs. Catherine ETA-NDU for photographs taken in St. Paul MN. She was a wonderful guide for me, Paul ETOGA, in the Twin Cities and in the biggest mall in the world, which is to be found here, the Mall of America.

Thanks also go to Mr. Michael BRENNA for photographs taken in Hawaii. I will never forget my trip to South Dakota with you who showed me the Badlands National Park and Mount Rushmore.

To Miss. Michiko NAKAGAWA for photographs taken in Hawaii and London U.K.,

To Mr. Hamid Bendouma for the photographs taken in the USA.

To Mr. Ray BROWN for the photographs taken in New York and New Jersey.

God Bless you all.

INTRODUCTION AND METHODOLOGY

The philosophy behind *ENGLISH FOR DAILY COMMUNICATION* is to show that, speaking a foreign language is rewarding, because it provides the learners with more job opportunities at home as well as abroad. It also allows them to travel and move through foreign milieus safely when the language barriers are removed or at least lessened. This additional ability to speak another language will give them an easier access to many varied cultures, interesting people, civilizations and leads to a much better understanding of those new environments.

Learning a foreign language is meaningful when the prime objective is to speak and communicate. In order to be able to speak fast and communicate effectively in English or any other foreign language, the learners need to have some degree of contact with the native speakers. The students should try to understand the native speakers' social life style, their history and the environments in which they have been molded. Only then, learning will become useful and enjoyable.

Learning English as a second language has never been an easy task, particularly when education is compulsory. Therefore, the teacher's main role should not be limited to correcting the student's mistakes, but to show how attractive the English language can be and give students an idea of the overall effort it will take to overcome the difficulties of pronunciation or the complexities of grammar as well in order to reach their goal.

There is no particular guidance for the teachers as for how to use this book, the layout is homogeneous and clear enough. However, after reading the conversation the teacher should as a matter of course ask questions such as: "Where does this conversation take place ?" "What is the conversation about ?" etc... in order to check the understanding of the conversation.

OBJECTIVES AND CONTAINS

The objectives of *ENGLISH FOR DAILY COMMUNICATION* are:

To provide the students with a useful textbook from which they can learn and appreciate the difference between American and British English. This approach allows them to be at ease while communicating with nationals of either countries.

To help the students become familiar with English by going through the many different kinds of exercises presented in the text. These same exercises should also help them get better results in language proficiency tests.

Each unit begins with a conversation, which gives students a common situation to think about and an example of authentic language used to communicate in such a situation. The topic of the conversation is used in the follow-up oral or written questions to encourage and extend the discussion. The students should also get used to making full sentences in their answers.

The grammar clearly presented in every unit, allows the student to understand how the language works. It is followed by various exercises to reinforce their understanding.

The reading passages in PART 3, **CULTURE AND CIVILIZATION**, are adapted from authentic sources. It presents the student who plans to study in the U.S.A or in the U.K a particular aspect of the American or British cultural experience and it may lead them to a deeper appreciation of the differences and similarities between their own culture, country and those of people from other lands.

CONTENTS

Part 3: Reading: Culture and Civilization
"Letters: inquiries and replies"
"Job Applications"
"Curriculum Vitae"

Appendix   141

Ⅰ. The Fifty Stars
Ⅱ. Irregular Verbs
Ⅲ. Measures and Weights
Ⅳ. Specialized Vocabularies
Ⅴ. Summary of Verb Tenses

Aloha ! We're in WAIKIKI, come and join us.

What a shot !

American VS British English

There are little differences between American and British English in grammar. However, the difference in vocabulary between the two is tremendous. Here is a foretaste of the differences you will learn about.

US	GB
mad	angry
anyplace	anywhere
fall	autumn
attorney	barrister or solicitor
chips	crisps (potato)
intersection	crossroad
closet	cupboard
tenderloin	fillet
movie	film
apartment	flat
flat, blow-out	flat tire, puncture
first floor	ground floor
ground meat	mince meat
purse, pocket-book	handbag
vacation	holiday(s)
elevator	lift
truck	lorry
stingy	mean
freeway, turnpike	motorway
mean	nasty, vicious
noplace	nowhere
sidewalk	pavement
gas or gasoline	petrol
baby carriage	pram
bar	pub, bar
coin-purse	purse

US	GB
railroad	railway
round trip	return ticket
collect call	reversed charge call
roadway	road surface, pavement
eraser	rubber
store	shop
one-way ticket	single ticket
someplace	somewhere
candy	sweets
faucet	tap
cab	taxi
sneakers	tennis shoes
can	tin
flashlight	torch
hobo	tramp
pants	trousers
subway	underground railway, tube
shorts	underpants
zipper	zip

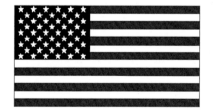

Unit 1

Would you like to order anything else ?

Part 1: Conversation

——————————— Breakfast ———————————

W: waitress   D: Dan   J: Jim   K: Kazuhiro

W: Good morning. Would you like a table or would you rather sit at the counter ?

D : How about the table over by the window ?

W: Certainly, wherever you like. Have a look at the menu and I will take your order in a minute.

D : Gee, everything looks good. What are you going to have guys ?

J : French toast for me, jam and hot milk tea.

K : I feel like having eggs with pancakes.

D : Why don't you have the special then ? You get juice, pancakes and choice of eggs.

K : That's a good idea.

W: Are you folks ready to order ?

D : Yes, we are. I'll have two toasts, scrambled eggs, well cooked, hot rolls and coffee.

K : Fried eggs for me, sunny-side up with the pancakes and an orange juice, please.

J : French toast for me, with strawberry jam and a cup of hot milk tea.

D : Could you hurry up a bit Miss, we're starving.

W: Sure. Coming right up.

I'm starving like Marvin.

Questions

1. Write a summary of the conversation above in a few lines. (no longer than six lines)

2. Answer the following questions.

   How many meals a day do you usually have ?
   At what time do you have your breakfast ? What is it always composed of ?

Exercises

A. Choose the correct answer.

   1. Would you like ....more tea ?
      a. some   b. any   c. no   d. few

   2. Shall I ....your order now ?
      a. call   b. turn   c. take   d. refuse

   3. Excuse me, I have knocked ....my cup of coffee. Would you wipe it up, please ?
      a. away   b. down   c. on   d. over

   4. We're out of muffins, would you care ....some donuts ?
      a. about   b. in   c. for   d. into

   5. Please stand here: the waitress will ....you soon.
      a. seat   b. take   c. bring   d. come

B. Translate the following sentences.

1. We serve breakfast until 11 a.m.

   ....

2. I'll have scrambled eggs with bacons and a side-order of hot rolls.

   ....

3. Is this table vacant ?

   ....

4. Miss, the check please !

   ....

5. Excuse me, could I change my order ?

   ....

Part 2: American VS British English

US	GB
gee	gosh
hash-brown potatoes	fried potatoes
hi !	hello !
sunny-side up	fried eggs
beverage	drinks
cookie	biscuit
sugar bowl	sugar basin
check	bill
sure	certainly

GRAMMAR

The Simple Present Tense

1. Statement

I / you / we / they **live**
in England.

He / she / it / **lives**
in England.

2. Negative

I / you / we / they **do not /
don't live** in England.

He / she / it / **does not /
doesn't live** in England.

3. Question

Do I / you / we / they **live**
in England ?

Does he / she / it **live**
in England ?

4. Short answer

Yes, you / I / we / they, **do**.
No, you / I / we / they **do not /
don't**
Yes, he / she / it **does**.
No, he / she / it **does not**.

5. Negative question

Don't I / you / we / they **live**
in England ?

Doesn't he, she, it **live**
in England ?

6. Answer

Yes, you / I / we / they **do**.
No, you / I / we / they / **do not /
don't**
Yes, he / she / it **does**.
No, he / she / it **does not**.

Rules: **1.** Use the simple present to talk about your habits or daily routine.
⇒Examples: I go to bed late every night.
Ken plays tennis on Sundays.

2. Use adverbs of frequency to show how often you do something or how often something happens. However, in a sentence, adverb of frequency can be placed: before the main verb, or after auxiliary verbs such as **be**, **have**, **can**, **will**, etc...
⇒Examples: I **often** run on Saturdays
Keiko speaks English, but she has **never** gone to the U.S.A.

YOUR TURN 1

Make a full sentence with each one of the following adverbs:
always, often, usually, sometimes, never, rarely, hardly ever, frequently, seldom.

....

....

....

....

....

....

....

....

....

....

YOUR TURN 2

Give the opposite of the following words.

proud.....................	broad.....................	patient.....................
different.....................	attentive.....................	enormous.....................
polite.....................	safe.....................	bright.....................
sweet.....................	handsome.....................	brave.....................

to be

1. Assertion		**2. Question**
I am /	I'm	am I ___?
You are /	you're	are you ___?
He / she / it is	he / she / it's	is he / she / it ___?
We are	we're	are we ___?
They are	they're	are they ___?

3. Negative

I **am not** or I'm not
You **are not** or you're not or you aren't
He / she / it **is not** or he / she / it**'s not** or he / she / it **isn't**
We **are not** or we**'re not** or we **aren't**
They **are not** or they**'re not** or they **aren't**

4. Negative questions

Am I not ___? or Ain't I ___?
Are you not ___? or Aren't you ___?
Is he / she / it not ___? or Isn't he / she / it ___?
Are we not ___? or Aren't we ___?
Are they not ___? or Aren't they ___?

to have

1. Assertion

I **have** or I**'ve**
You **have** or you**'ve**
He / she / it **has** or he / she / it**'s**
We **have** or we**'ve**
They **have** or they**'ve**

2. Question

have I ___?
have you ___?
has he / she / it ___?
have we ___?
have they ___?

3. Negative

I **have not** or I **haven't**
You **have not** or you **haven't**
He / she / it **has not** or he / she / it **hasn't**
We **have not** or we **haven't**
They **have not** or they **haven't**

4. Negative questions

Have I **not** ___? or **Haven't** I ___?
Have you **not** ___? or **Haven't** you ___?
Has he / she / it **not** ___? or **Hasn't** he / she / it ___?
Have we **not** ___? or **Haven't** we ___?
Have they **not** ___? or **Haven't** they ___?

Part 3
Reading: Culture and Civilization

───────── **English and American Breakfast** ─────────

The traditional English breakfast is mainly composed of fried eggs, bacon, tea, toast, jam or marmalade. However, it is now very common to see cereals served. Coffee is also taking over the dominance of tea.

In the United States, breakfast is considered a substantial meal designed to carry you on through the day, as many workers have only a light lunch. An American breakfast can include juice, hot or cold cereal, eggs, sausages, toasts and pancakes. The usual beverage is coffee, tea or milk.

● **Brunch:**

A brunch is a combination of breakfast and lunch that many Americans enjoy on Sundays.

Now this is what I call a breakfast !

Unit 2

May I see your boarding pass and your passport please ?

Part 1: Conversation

──────── Going to the States ────────

FA: Flight Attendant   K : Kazu   B: Bob

Announcement: The United Airlines flight number UA 4400 to Los Angeles is now boarding at gate 36. In order to avoid delays, all passengers must proceed immediately. We thank you for your cooperation.

B : Come on, Kazu, our flight is now boarding at gate 36. Let's go.

K : Don't worry. I'll take only a minute to buy a gift for a friend of mine.

B : Well, hurry up then. It'd be a shame to miss the plane now.

K : O.K. I'm done now. Sorry for making you nervous.

B : Get our boarding passes ready.

FA : Hello. May I have your boarding passes please ?

K : Here you are.

FA : Your seats will be on the left side of the plane, row H.

B : Kazu, would you like the window or the aisle seat ?

K : Do you mind if I sit by the aisle ? I'd just as soon be able to get up and go to the toilets or walk around.

B : Of course not. I wonder if we can order drinks now. Excuse me Miss !

FA: Yes ?

B : We'd like to order drinks.

FA : I'm sorry. You'll have to wait until the plane takes off to be served. Please fasten your seat belt, we are about to take off.

B : Sure.

Victoria Station

Questions

1. Write a small summary of the conversation above. (no longer than six lines)

2. Answer the following questions.

   Do you like to travel ?
   How many times a year do you go away ? Do you fly ?

Exercises

A. Choose the correct answer.

   1. Your bag is too big, Bob ! It won't fit.........the overhead compartment.
      a. by   b. onto   c. in   d. over

   2. Try .... it under the seat.
      a. by slide   b. sliding   c. slide   d. to slide

   3. My earphones ....work.
      a. doesn't   b. don't   c. can't   d. can

   4. These seats are unreserved. Please sit ....you like.
      a. by   b. where   c. down   d. over

   5. Would you mind ....over one seat ?
      a. to move   b. moved   c. moving   d. by moving

B. Translate the following sentences.

   1. We are flying over Hokkaido at the moment.

   ....

2. Our flight is one hour late.

....

3. The sun is bothering me. Could you pull the curtain ?

....

4. This plane is taking off on schedule.

....

5. Excuse me, do you have any Japanese newspapers ?

....

Part 2: American VS British English

US	GB
movie	film
aisle	gangway
sure	certainly

GRAMMAR

The Present Progressive Tense

Rules: 1. The present progressive is formed with **be** + **present participle** (**ing**) of the main verb.

   2. Use the present progressive to describe or to talk about an action that is happening at the time of speaking.

1. Statement

I am (I'm) listening.

You are (you're) listening.

2. Negative

I am not (I'm not) listening.

You are not (you're not) listening.

He (he's) / she (she's) / it (it's) is listening.

He / she / it is not (isn't) listening.

We are (we're) listening.

We are not (aren't) listening.

They are (they're) listening.

They are not (aren't) listening.

3. Question

Am I listening ?

Are you listening ?

Is he / she / it listening ?

Are we listening ?

Are you listening ?

Are they listening ?

4. Short answer

Yes, you are.
No, you are not (aren't).
Yes, I am.
No, I am not.
Yes, he / she / it is.
No, he / she / it is not (isn't).
No, he's / she's / it's not.
Yes, you are.
No, you are not (you're not).
Yes, we are.
No, we are not (we're not).
Yes, they are.
No, they are not (they're not).

5. Negative Questions

Am I not listening ?

Aren't you listening ?

Isn't he / she / it listening ?

Aren't we listening ?

Aren't you listening ?

6. Answer

Yes, you are.
No, you are not (you're not).
Yes, I am.
No, I am not (I'm not).

Yes, he / she / it is.
No, he / she / it is not (isn't).
No, he's / she's / it's not.

Yes, you are.
No, you are not (you're not).
Yes, we are.
No, we are not (we're not).

Aren't they listening ?

Yes, they are.

No, they are not (they're not).

3. Verbs that describe states or situations that are not expected to change are not usually used in the progressive.

Verbs that describe the senses:

to hear, to see, to smell, to taste

⇒Example: This apple tastes good.

Verbs that express feelings and emotion:

to dislike, to hate, to like, to love, to prefer, to want

⇒Example: Mike hates bowling, but Cristie loves it.

Verbs that express possession:

to have, to belong, to own, to possess

⇒Example: We own all these houses.

verbs that express beliefs, opinion, and knowledge:

to believe, to think, to know, to understand

⇒Example: Everyone in my family believes in God.

More non progressive verbs:

to be, to cost, to exist, to need, to owe

⇒Example: My father needs a new car. His old BMW is already falling apart.

YOUR TURN 1

Make full sentences with the following verbs.

to prefer, to see, to hear, to think, to understand, to possess, to seem, to exist, to cost

....

....

....

....

....

....

....

....

....

YOUR TURN 2

Give synonyms for the following words.

beautiful......................	difficult......................	expensive......................
clever......................	nice......................	rich......................
kind......................	grateful......................	unhappy......................

Exercises

A. Complete the following sentences with the simple present or the present progressive, using the verbs in parentheses.

1. Hello Jack, lend me 50 bucks, I..................to pay you back next week. (to promise)

2. Watch out ! There ....a bull ....behind you ! (to be, to come)

3. Look outside Mary ....it......................? (to rain)

4. How many hours.................you.................per week ? (to work)

5. How often.................your mother.................for your family ? (to cook)

6. The sun ....in the east and ....in the west. (to rise, to set)

7. Every year, I ....my girl friend flowers for her birthday, but she always.................mine. (to send, to forget)

8. Listen to what the teacher.................It ....interesting for once. (to say, to sound)

9. - What's wrong Dan ? ....something.................you ? (to bother)
   - Yes, a bit.
   - Tell me about it. I can help you. That............what friends ....for, right ? (to be)
   - My rent............ due tomorrow but I ....a penny in my bank account right now. Can you help me out ? (to be, not to have)
   - Well, go to your bank and ask for a loan. I............, too. (to be broke)

10. It is time to go shopping for groceries ....you.................with me ? (to come)

11. Mark............a letter, ...him. (to write, not to disturb)

12. He.................the paper every morning before he.................to work. (to read, to go)

13. Everybody............the summer time. (to like)

14. I must go, my wife............for me now. (to wait)

Where's my ticket ?

Part 3
Reading: Culture and Civilization

—————————The Birth of the United States—————————

Sequences

1492. Christopher Colombus discovers the New World.

1607. Captain John Smith establishes the first British colony at Jamestown (Virginia)

1763. The Treaty of Paris ends French control east of the Mississippi.

1776. July 4th is declared Independence Day.

1783. Britain acknowledges the independence of the United States of America.

1788. The Constitution is adopted.

1789. George Washington is elected the first president of the United States.

1803. Louisiana is purchased from France for about $15 million (70 million French francs)

1861. The Civil War begins at Fort Sumter on April 12 and ends on April 12, 1865.

Source: Adapted from the *USA in your Pocket* D. ENGLE

Let's reach for the stars !

Excuse me sir, how do I get to Green Park from here ?

Unit 3

Enjoy yourself in the big city but don't be careless !

Part 1: Conversation

——————————Reporting a Lost Passport——————————

A: Agent   M: Michael

A : Hello. May I help you ?

M: Yes, I have come to report a missing passport.

A : I see. What's your passport number ?

M: Well, I think it is GB / 798099.

A : When and where was it issued ?

M: 07 / 2004 in London.

A : I'll need to ask you for a few more details. First of all, your full name and address.

M: It's Michael Brenna. B-R-E-N-N-A

40 Canons Hill

Old Coulsdon

Surrey 1HB CR5

UK

A : Thank you. Now, did you say the passport was lost or stolen ?

M: Certainly stolen, and due to carelessness on my part, I'm afraid. It must have fallen in the fitting room when I went to try on a jacket. It was only an hour later that I realized that I didn't have my passport any more.

A : Are there any other papers missing ?

M: Fortunately, nothing else is missing. I always keep my credits cards and my passport separately.

A : We will investigate. Then the necessary steps will be taken to have a new passport issued to you.

M: Thank you ever so much.

A : You are welcome.

Questions

1. Write a summary of the conversation above in a few lines (no longer than six lines).

2. Answer the following questions.

   Have you ever lost something ?
   What was it ?
   Did you report it ?
   Where did you report it ?
   Did you get it back ?

Exercises

A. Choose the correct answer.

1. I ....here to report a lost credit card.
   a. be   b. being   c. have been   d. am

2. I have ....notified the police.
   a. yet   b. still   c. already   d. early

3. My card is outdated. It ....May 2nd.
   a. is expiring   b. has expired   c. will expire   d. expired

4. How soon will my new card be............?
   a. issuing   b. issued   c. issue   d. have issued

5. I don't have an American Express Card. Would you............ Visa ?
   a. have accepted   b. be accepted   c. accept   d. accepting

B. Translate the following sentences.

1. Can you specify whether your passport has been lost or stolen ?

   ....

2. What happens if someone's been using my credit card ?

   ....

3. What should I do to have another passport issued ?

   ....

4. In Japan, most travel agencies do not accept credit cards payment.

   ....

5. What is your credit card expiration date ?

   ....

Part 2: American VS British English

US	GB
Checkbook	cheque book
Bathrobe	dressing gown
Grubs	old, very casual clothes
Nightgown	nightdress
Panty hose	tights
Pants	trousers
Pea jacket	navy style duffel coat
Tuxedo	dinner jacket
Undershirt	vest
Vest	waistcoat
Pumps	dancing shoes

GRAMMAR

A. The Simple Past

1. Statement
I / you / he / she / we / they
went to New York.

I / you / he / she / it / we / they
arrived in New York.

2. Negative
I / you / he / she / it / we / they
did not go to New York.

I / you / he / she / it / we / they
did not arrive in New York.

3. Question
Did I / you / he / she / it /
we / they **go** to New York ?

4. Short answer
Yes, you / I / he / she / it /
we / they **did**.
No, you / I / he / she / it /
we / they **did not** / **didn't**.

5. Negative Questions
Didn't I / you / he / she / it /
we / they go to New York ?

6. Answer
Yes, you / I / he / she / it /
we / they **did**
No, you / I / he / she / it /
we / they **did not** / **didn't**.

Rules: Use the simple past to talk or tell about an action that started and finished in the past. See irregular verbs. (See P.143~)

YOUR TURN 1

Complete the following sentences by using the verbs in parentheses in the past tense.

1. Mum (feed)................the dog early this morning. I (can't do)................ it because I (do not) ....have enough time.
2. In Japan the typhoon (destroy)................hundreds of houses last month.
3. It (be not)..............necessary to run, we (have)..............enough time to catch the train.

4. Mr. Smith (grow).................a moustache to impress his children.

5. My father (teach).................French at Oxford University a few years ago. He (write)..............and (publish)...............many books.

6. I (visit)..............the Aero-Space Museum in Washington D.C. in 1990. It (be).........very interesting.

7. An alligator (escape).................from a Florida zoo two weeks ago during a hurricane.

   - I hope it (do not)............ eat anyone or someone's pet.

   - Yeah! I hope so too. At least no one (be declare)...............missing after it (be capture)..............

   - Who (catch)..............it ?

   - The police (do)............... I (watch)...............it on TV.

B. The Past Progressive

1. Statement

I / he / she / it **was working**

We / you / they **were working.**

2. Negative

I / he / she / it was not / **wasn't working.**

We / you / they were not / **weren't working.**

3. Question

Was I / he / she / it **working ?**

Were we / you / they **working ?**

4. Short answer

Yes, you **were**; he / she / it **was**.
   You / they **were** / I **was**.
No, you **were not** / **weren't**
   He / she / it **was not** / **wasn't**.
I **was not** / **wasn't** / they **were not** / **weren't**.

Rules: Use the past progressive to tell about an action that was in progress at one specific moment or time in the past.

Exercises

Complete the following sentences using the words in parentheses. Use the simple past or the past progressive or the past perfect.

1. This morning, I (go) ....to the post office to get some stamps.
2. On my way, I (meet) ....an old friend of mine, Jerome. He (wait) ....for the bus.
3. As the bus (be)...............late, we just (stand)...............there and (talk) .... about old times.
4. He (tell) ....me about how much he (like) ....his job and he (earn)...............a lot of money. He (look)...............happy and healthy.
5. While we (be talk) ...., we (realize) ....that we (have not) ....seen each other for almost five years.
6. He (have change not) ....and he (be delighted) ....to see me again, so (be) ....I.
7. Unfortunately, the bus (arrive)............... and he (have)...............to go. When he (get)................on the bus steps, he (turn back) .... (raise) ....his right hand and (wave)...............at me.
8. Right before he (get)...............on the bus, we (exchange) ....our phone numbers and (promise)...............each other to meet again soon.

YOUR TURN 2

Give the opposite of the following words.

tall.....................	high.....................	careful.....................
fat..........................	generous.....................	similar.....................
educated................	long.....................	useful.....................

Part 3
Reading: Culture and Civilization

──────────────**One Island, Three Countries**──────────────

The nation of Great Britain is made of three countries: England, Wales and Scotland. The United Kingdom (UK) consists of Great Britain, Northern Ireland and some other islands such as the Isle of Man and the Channel Isles.

The Isle of Man is located between Wales and Ireland and the Channel Islands are located between England and France.

Here is a quick overview of the island of Britain's landscape: England, 50,000 sq miles, is the largest of the three political divisions. Scotland, 30,000 sq miles is in the north and Wales 8,000 sq miles is in the west.

The island of Ireland consists of Northern Ireland and the Republic of Ireland, also known as Eire. The Republic of Ireland, with Dublin as its capital, is a completely separate country from the other. Thus, the term British Isles designates geographically the whole group of islands that make up the UK and the Republic of Ireland.

Source: Adapted from *Britain*, Lonely planet

Do they still use double-decker buses in London ?

Unit 4

Palm trees, the sun, the beach... this is the greatest place.

Part 1: Conversation

At the Hotel

R: receptionist   M: Mark   L: Linda

R : Hi ! How can I help you ?

M: I was wondering if you'd have a room available for the two of us.

R : Have you made a reservation ?

M: Not really, but...

R : Let me check the computer. I'm afraid the hotel is full at the moment. It's the holiday season, you know.

L : Mark, I told you we should have made a reservation. Where are we going to spend the night now ?

M: Yes, you're right. I have been a little bit careless. Let me talk to the manager, he might be able to do something. Excuse me Sir !

R : Yes, what can I do for you ?

M: I perfectly understand that you're all booked up, but I'd be grateful if you could manage something for us, at least for tonight. My wife is pregnant.

R : Well, in that case all I can offer you is our Royal Suite room with a king-size bed, only for tonight.

M: What are the rates on your rooms ?

R : That will be $500 with, cable TV, air-conditioning, dinner and breakfast included. How long were you planning to stay ?

L : Three nights. But I'm afraid we haven't got much choice, we'd better take it.

R : If something cheaper opens up tomorrow, we'll let you know. Here is your key. It'll be room 306. The porter will show you the way.

Questions

1. Write a summary of the conversation above in a few lines. (no longer than six lines)

2. Answer the following questions.

> Have you ever stayed in a hotel ?
> How long did you stay there ?
> Do you remember its name ?
> Who did the booking for you ?

Exercises

A. Choose the correct answer.

1. You see, I told you we should............reservations.
    a. make   b. have making   c. have made   d. can make

2. Oh ! I almost.............to take the key for our room.
    a. forgotten   b. forgot   c. forgetting   d. have forgotten

3. We were planning ....the day after tomorrow.
    a. for leave   b. leaving   c. to leave   d. leaved

4. I'm afraid we ....much choice.
    a. getting   b. have gotten   c. haven't got   d. got

5. I'll have you.............to the airport tomorrow morning.
    a. drove   b. driving   c. driven   d. drive

6. Can you have a cup of tea ....to my room ?
    a. send   b. sended   c. sending   d. sent

B. Translate the following sentences.

1. Hello, I'm Ted Johnson I made a reservation a couple of days ago.

   ....

2. Yes, Mr. Johnson we were expecting you.

   ....

3. I booked for two nights, but I plan to stay three more nights.

   ....

4. We are a bit early. Is there anywhere we can leave our luggage ?

   ....

5. I'm checking out tomorrow morning. Can you cash travelers checks ?

   ....

6. What time does the restaurant close at night ?

   ....

Part 2: American VS British English

US	GB
regular	normal, standard
queen-size	king-size (d), de luxe
bell-boy	page-boy

GRAMMAR

The Present Perfect

1. Statement

I / you / we / they
   have ('ve) eaten.
He / she / it / **has ('s) eaten.**

2. Negative

I / you / we / they
   have not (haven't) eaten.
He / she / it has **not (hasn't) eaten.**

3. Question

Have I / you / we / they **eaten ?**

Has he / she / it **eaten ?**

4. Short answer

Yes, you / I / we / they **have.**
No, you / I / we / they
   have not (haven't).

Yes, he / she / it **has.**
No, he / she / it **has not (hasn't).**

5. Negative Question

Haven't I / you / we / they
   eaten ?

Hasn't he / she / it **eaten ?**

6. Answer

Yes, you / I / we / they **have.**
No, you / I / we / they **have not
   (haven't).**

Yes, he / she / it has.
No, he / she / it **has not (hasn't).**

Rules: 1. Use the present perfect (have, has + past participle) to tell about something that began in the past and that continues to the present.
  ⇒Examples: I **have worked** in this company for ten years.
   He **has been** here for hours.

  2. Use the present perfect progressive **(have/has + been + verb + ing),** to tell or talk about something or an activity that is so recent that you can still see or feel the result.
  ⇒Examples: I **have been eating**. (The plate is still on the table.) He **has been running**. (He is still sweating.)

3. Use the present perfect to tell about an action or a situation that began in the past and is continuing up to the present time.

⇒Examples: I **have been waiting** for the bus for half an hour.
My sister **has been talking** on the phone for the last hour.

4. Use the present perfect when no time in the past is specified.

⇒Examples: **Have you finished** your work ? No, **I haven't finished** yet.

5. Use the present perfect to talk about the first of two actions in the future.

⇒Examples: When I **have finished** my work, I am going out.

YOUR TURN

A. Use the present perfect in the following sentences.

1. Someone / to steal /my bike.

....

2. She / not / to think about you.

....

3. You / to lose / my umbrella ?

....

4. The train / not / to arrive / yet.

....

5. They / to find / their missing cat ?

....

6. Bob / not / to speak / to his wife for months.

....

7. You / not / to show / me your new watch.

....

B. Use the simple past tense or the past progressive or the past perfect or the past perfect progressive or the present perfect or the present perfect progressive to complete the following sentences.

1. In Japan, an earthquake (destroy).................... thousands of houses in 1995.
2. This shop (sell)....................lots of items until the manager changed.
3. Mr. Clay (teach)......................English at Kaetsu University for ten years.
4. - (finish)....................your homework ?
   - Yes, I have.
   - Then, you can have a rest now.
5. I (feed)....................the dog. We can leave now.
6. Since I (move)....................to this neighborhood, I (make)................ a lot of friends.

C. Same exercise.

1. You deserve a good rest, you (work)....................a lot for the last two days.
2. Why don't we have a rest ? We (work)....................a lot yesterday.
3. A week ago, I (work)....................so hard that I had to take a day off afterwards.
4. He (work)....................too much, he needs a rest.

D. Same exercise.

1. My mother (make)....................some nice cookies for my dad's birthday. They were so tasty !
2. I (make)....................cookies for three hours, I'd better stop now.
3. She (make)....................cookies for about half an hour, but She had to stop to answer the phone.
4. Since I am the one who (make)................the cookies, you should go and get the drinks for the guests.

Part 3
Reading: Culture and Civilization

——————African Americans in the U.S.A——————

Sequences and chronology

1775 - The first anti-slavery organization group was founded in Pennsylvania.

1791 - Ely Whitney invents the cotton-gin, cotton plantations spread out and the need for slaves increases.

1820 - Congress rules that all new territory north, of the border between North Carolina and Tennessee will be "free"; all territory to the south of that border is left open to future slavery.

1865 - Congress ratifies the 13th Amendment: *"Neither slavery nor involuntary servitude, except as a punishment for crime whereof* (wherefrom = from which) *the party shall have been duly convicted, shall exist within the United States, or any place subject to their jurisdiction,"*

1866 - The 16th Amendment extends civil rights to Negroes.

1910 - The NAACP (National Association for the Advancement of Colored People) is founded in New York. The "Great Migration" of the southern Blacks toward the North begins. The Southern States publish the "Black Codes" in order to restrict the freedom of emancipated slaves.

1954 - Supreme Court outlaws racial discrimination in public schools.

1955 - Martin Luther King creates the *non-violent* S.C.L.C. (Southern Christian Leadership Conference) in order to protest against discrimination in public transportation), in Montgomery (Ala.)

1957 - In Little Rock (Ark.), paratroopers and National Guardsmen must intervene to impose integration of Negro children in local schools.

1963 - Medgar Evers, leader of NAACP, is murdered in Jackson (Miss.). There is widespread violence against the Negroes throughout the South.

1963 - (Aug. 28) March on Washington : 200,000 black and white demonstrators from all parts of the USA gather on the steps of the

Lincoln Memorial to demand civil rights for the Negroes.

1964 - Congress votes for the Civil Rights Act initiated by President J.F. Kennedy. It guarantees voting rights to the Negroes and prohibits segregation in public accommodations and facilities.

1965 - Malcolm X, former leader of the Black Muslims is assassinated in New York City.

1968 - (April 4) Dr Martin Luther King is shot by a sniper in Memphis (Tenn.)

Source: Adapted from the *USA in your pocket* D. Engle

Aloha !

Greetings from the city that never sleeps. Come and join us !

Unit 5

Department stores are crowded at Christmas time.

Merry Christmas everybody !

Part 1: Conversation

──────────── Shopping ────────────

M: Martha   C: Christie

M: Hi, Christie. I haven't seen you for awhile! How have you been ?

C : Not bad, I have been busy studying for my driving license test.

M: So, how did it go ?

C : Lousy. I lost control of the car during the driving test and we almost crashed.

M: Oh ! That's too bad. Listen, I was thinking of going downtown to have a look at the sales. How would you like to come along ? It might help you to change your mind.

C : Yeah ! Ok. Are you going to drive ?

M: Sure. I can give you free driving lessons on the way there.

C : Great ! I tell you what, give me half an hour, just to take a shower and get dressed.

M: All right. I'll pick you up in front of your house in thirty minutes.

(Downtown, at a Department Store)

C : Look at how crowded this place is ! I wonder if there is something decent left.

M: This is Christmas, you know. Let's take a look at the directory over there.

C : Let's see, first floor...cosmetics, lingerie. Second floor...ladies clothing. Third floor...men, records.... Fourth floor, computer software... housewares... furniture.

M: Let's go to ladies clothing first, we'll look for gifts later.

C : This jacket is gorgeous. I think I'll try it on. Well, what do you think ?

M: It looks great on you, and it is half price.

C : Thanks. I'll take it.

Questions

1. Write a summary of the conversation above in a few lines. (no longer than six lines)

2. Answer the following questions.

   Do you like shopping ?

   How often do you go shopping ? Where ?

   Check out about the Mall of America: what can you tell about it ?

   Where is it located (at) ?

Exercises

A. Choose the correct answer.

1. Mum, have a look ....my new dress. What do you think ?
   a. on　　　　b. for　　　　c. in　　　　d. at

2. In this store, computers can be found ....the second floor.
   a. at　　　　b. in　　　　c. on　　　　d. by

3. Excuse me, I'm ....trousers for men. Where can I find them ?
   a. look for　　b. looking at　　c. looking for　　d. look at

4. I'm afraid we're all ....of your size.
   a. selling　　b. sell out　　c. sold out　　d. sold

5. The fitting rooms are ....there.
   a. by　　　　b. at　　　　c. over　　　　d. in

B. Translate the following sentences.

1. Excuse me sir, could you tell me where the ladies' department is ?

....

2. This black jacket looks nice. May I try it on ?

....

3. How much is it ? There's no price tag on it.

....

4. I can't afford it. It is too expensive.

....

5. Can you gift-wrap this watch for me please ?

....

6. What time do stores close in Tokyo ?

....

Part 2: American VS British English

US	GB
first floor	ground floor
second floor	first floor
pants	trousers
underpants	pants
housewares	household goods

GRAMMAR

The Future Tense with *Will*

1. Statement
I / you / we / they /
      will / **'ll** work.

He / she / it **will** / **'ll** work.

2. Negative
I / you / we / they /
      will not / **won't** work.

He / she / it **will not** /
      won't work.

3. Question
Will I / you / we / they work ?

Will he / she / it work ?

4. Short answer
Yes, you / I / we / they **will**.
No, you / I / we / they
      will not / **won't**.

Yes, he / she / it **will**.
No, he / she / it **will not** / **won't**.

5. Negative Question
Won't I / you / we / they work ?

Won't he / she / it work ?

6. Answer
Yes, You / I / we / they **will**.
No, you / I / we / they
      will not / **won't**.
Yes, he / she / it **will**.
No, he / she / it **will not** / **won't**.

Rules:
1. Use **will** in formal situation to talk or tell about something in the future.
   ⇒Example: The President **will** address the nation tomorrow.

2. Use **will** to make a promise.
   ⇒Example: I **will** / **'ll** never tell you a lie.

The Future Tense with *Be Going to*

1. Statement

I **am** / **'m going to** work.
You / we / they / **are**
          going to work.
He / she / it **is going to** work.

2. Negative

I **am** / **'m not going to** work.
You / we / they / **are not** / **aren't**
          going to work.
He / she / it **is not** /
          isn't going to work.

3. Question

Am I **going to** work ?

Are you **going to** work ?

Are we / they **going to** work ?

Is he / she / it **going to** work ?

4. Short answer

Yes, you **are**.
No, you **are not** / **aren't**.

Yes, I **am**.
No, I **am not**.
Yes, you / we / they **are**.
No, we / they **are not** / **aren't**.

Yes, he / she / it **is**.
No, he / she / it **is not** / **isn't**.

5. Negative Question

Am I not **going to** work ?

Aren't you **going to** work ?

Aren't we / they **going to**
          work ?
Isn't he / she / it **going to**
          work ?

6. Answer

Yes, you **are**.
No, you **are not** / **aren't**.

Yes, I **am**.
No, I **am not**.
Yes, you / we / they **are**.
No, we / they **are not** / **aren't**.
Yes, he / she / it **is**.
No, he / she / it **is not** / **isn't**

Rules: Use **be going to** (also pronounced ***gonna***) in an informal speech or any other situation, to talk about something that will happen in the future, or soon.

⇒Example: I did not study hard. I think **I'm going to** fail my English test.

My brother is a good singer. One day, He **is going to** be a pop star.

YOUR TURN 1

A. Write about your future plans using will or be going to.

....
....
....
....
....
....
....

B. Complete the following conversations, using *be going to, 'll or will*.

1. A: The idea of moving to a new apartment gives me a headache.
   B: I see what you're talking about. But don't worry I................help you.

2. A: Really ? That's great. ....you also help me to clean the apartment ?
   B: Uh...I...............see what I can do. But I ....to promise you anything now.

3. A: Joe, don't forget that you still owe me 30 bucks from yesterday shopping.
   B: Stop harassing me with that, Bob. Didn't I say that I .... to pay you back tomorrow ?

4. A: We ....to the theater this evening. Are you coming with us ?
   B: I'm afraid I can't. I....................have to work late.

YOUR TURN 2

Give the plural of the following words.

ox...............	duty....................	loaf.....................
thief......................	potato...............	monkey.................
volcano................	goose....................	roof...............
person..................	swine....................	food......................
fish.................	music.................	milk.....................
workman...............	train...............	hair................
luggage.................	furniture....................	news................
match.................	box......................	glass................
clock.................	baby...................	knife................
cliff....................	wife....................	wolf..................
country...............	mouse....................	tooth................
woman................	sheep.................	deer....................
tomato...............	factory.................	life....................
house...................		

The VIP section

Part 3
Reading: Culture and Civilization

──────────────── London City ────────────────

London, a dynamic city, counts nearly 12 million inhabitants. These people belong to several ethnic groups and they all live in harmony.

Known as a city with magnificent historical architecture, its most familiar landmarks are Big Ben, the Tower of London, and the River Thames.

It is said that, although the Celts were the first to establish themselves at a ford crossing the River Thames, it was the Romans who developed the City of London as it is known today. They built a bridge and an amazing city wall, transformed the area into the hub of their road system in Britain.

When the Romans abandoned Britain in the 5th century, the Saxons moved in, organized the town by dividing it into 20 different wards. The Vikings attacked and defeated the Saxons, and the Danish leader, Canute became the King of England early in the 11th century. After his death, the Throne reverted to the Saxons. Edward the Confessor was consecrated and died a week later in 1065.

The city was then invaded by the Normans led by William the Conqueror who was crowned king. He built the White Tower (the Tower of London).

Then, the Throne passed through various houses in the following millennium. Since 1910, it has been in the House of Windsor, but political power has been concentrated in London.

Source: Adapted from *Britain*, Lonely planet.

Let's have lunch here and then we can go to see Big Ben.

Unit 6

I'm glad you could make it.
Do you know everybody here ?

Part 1: Conversation

———————————— At the Party ————————————

S: Susan   J: John   T: Tony

S : Hi, everyone. I'm glad you could make it to the party.

J : Hi, Susan. This is my younger brother, Tony. He lives in Japan. He is on vacation here in Bethesda at the moment, so I brought him along. I thought you wouldn't mind.

S : Of course not. Hi, Tony. Nice to meet you. I've heard so much about you.

Please, I'd like you to tell me about life in Japan.

T : Nice to meet you too. I wonder what my brother told you about me.

S : Well, come on in. I'll introduce you to the other guests. Then, I'll show you around the house.

J : Susan, what a lovely house ! How long have you been living here ?

S : About a year, I guess. We moved in last summer and we haven't stopped working on it ever since.

T : I like your terrace. Did you do it yourselves or did you have it done ?

S : My brother and his friends did it in their spare time. They also did the fence around the back garden.

J : What's that? Is that the solar heating ?

S : Yeah. We had it put in because we needed to cut down on the electricity bill.

T : You must save a lot on the heating.

S : We certainly do. Well, we'd better get back to the guests. I hope everyone's enjoying themselves. Help yourselves to a drink, you two. There's beer, iced-tea, orange juice etc...

J : That's a good idea.

Questions

1. Write a summary of the conversation above in a few lines. (no longer than six lines)

2. Answer the following questions.

Tell us about the place where you live.

> Do you live in a house or in an apartment (US) / a flat (GB) ?
> How big is it ?
> How long have you been living there ?
> How far is it from the station ? What is the name of your station ?
> Which line is it on ?
> How do you get to the station ?
> How long does it take you to go to school or work ?

Exercises

A. Choose the correct answer.

1. I thought I................the bell ring. It must be John.
   a. to hear   b. heard.   c. have heard   d. am hearing

2. Paul, thanks for.............to my party.
   a. you have come   b. came   c. you came   d. coming

3. I'm looking forward to ....soon.
   a. have to hear you.   b. hear you
   c. hearing from you.   d. be able to hear

4. Do you think John will come to our party tonight ? – I hope..........
   a. no   b. not   c. not so   d. that not

5. Come and spend the week-end with us ! – I'd like...........

      a. it   b. so   c. I would   d. to

B. Translate the following sentences.

1. Can you come over for dinner ?

....

2. What time shall I come ?

....

3. Terribly sorry I'm late. I was stuck in the traffic jam.

....

4. My car broke down in the middle of the highway yesterday. I was so embarrassed.

....

5. So, did you fix it or did you have it fixed ?

....

6. There is nothing I could have done by myself, so I had to be towed.

....

7. That must have cost you a lot of money.

....

Part 2: American VS British English

US	GB
hi !	hello !
nice to meet you	pleased to meet you
den	living-room
sure	certainly

GRAMMAR

Passive and Active voice

Forming the passive

Examples: (1) with **be** and **help**

Tense	**Form**
Simple present:	I **am helped**.
Present progressive:	I **am being helped**.
Simple past:	I **was helped**.
Past progressive:	I **was being helped**.
Present perfect:	I **have been helped**.
Past perfect:	I **had been helped**.
Future (will):	I **will be helped**.
Future (be going to)	I **am going to be helped**.
Future perfect:	I **will have been helped**.
Conditional	I **would be helped**.
(past)	I **would have been helped**.

Examples: (2)

Active: They found him in the garden.

Passive: He was found in the garden.

Rules: Use the active form to show your focus on the one who performs the action. Then, use the passive to show your focus on the result of the action and not the one performing it.

YOUR TURN 1

A. Turn the following sentences into passive voice.

1. Someone will tell him.

....

2. They taught her English well.

....

3. They interviewed me yesterday.

....

4. They have put up the ticket prices.

....

5. The typhoon blew the roof of the house off.

....

6. Someone offered them money.

....

7. They told him to keep quiet.

....

8. Nobody ever feeds the cats.

....

9. We all mourned Princess Diana's death.

....

B. Turn the following sentences into active voice.

1. She was sent a love letter.

....

2. I was told to shut up in class.

....

3. We will be served some good tea.

....

4. She is asked to sing.

....

5. We are told to sit down.

....

YOUR TURN 2

Continue these:

1. A cat mews
2. A dog ....
3. A pig.............................
4. A cow............................
5. A hen............................
6. A donkey.....................
7. A lion ....
8. A frog...........................
9. An elephant................
10. An owl.........................
11. A horse.......................
12. A sheep.......................

We had a great time. Please visit us again.

Part 3
Reading: Culture and Civilization

——————Washington D.C. (The Nation's Capital)——————

The city of Washington, officially called "the District of Columbia" (D.C.) is located 230 miles southwest of New York. This city covers 70 square miles and it is divided into 4 sections (N.E. – N.W. – S.E. – S.W.) the center of which is the Capitol Building.

In 1800, Washington became the nation's capital, the center of the Federal Government, seat of the President, Congress and Supreme Court.
The Federal Government is therefore the main "industry" for most of its inhabitants, nearly 80% of whom are Black.

It is said that the location of Washington D.C. had been picked out by George Washington himself, on the banks of the Potomac River, not far from his Virginia home. Washington also chose the architect and planner for the city, a Frenchman by the name of Pierre l'Enfant. The best place to appreciate the grandeur of Washington's layout is from the top of the Washington Monument.

What to see in Washington D.C.
- The White House
- The Lincoln and Jefferson Memorials
- The Capitol, home of the Congress.
- The National Gallery of Arts
- The Aero-Space Museum

Not far from this area are:
- Arlington Cemetery (graves of John and Robert Kennedy)
- The Pentagon
- Georgetown, a delightful old English town, with tree-lined cobbled streets, Georgian-style houses and boutiques.

Source: Adapted from the U.S.T.S. Brochure, *USA Northeast Travel Guide*

Unit 7

I've got to go to the bank.
Tomorrow is the start of the long weekend.

Part 1: Conversation

─────────── **At the Bank** ───────────

T: Teller   G: George   K: Kazuhiro

G : Kazu, the bank will soon close. We'd better hurry if you want to cash your traveler's.

K : I see what you mean. How far do we have to go ?

G : The bank is two blocks away from here, and it'll be closing in 20 minutes. We should make it on time, if we run.

K : We're cutting it a bit close. I haven't got much cash left for the weekend.

G : Excuse me, we'd like to cash some traveler's checks.

T : Next window, sir...

K : Can you cash these traveler's please ?

T : Certainly. Please sign your name on each of the checks and do not forget the date. Can I have your I.D card or driver's license ?

K : Will my passport do ?

T : Sure. How would you want that ? Tens, twenties, fifties, hundreds ?

K : Five tens and four fifties will be fine, please.

T : Here you are.

K : Thank you. George, didn't you want to withdraw some money ?

G : Yes, but that is not a problem. I'll do it from an A.T.M outside the building.

K : Thanks to you, I managed to cash my travelers.

G : Hey, any time.

You must go see
Buckingham Palace.
Its big, isn't it !

Questions

1. Write a summary of the conversation above in a few lines. (no longer than six lines.

2. Answer the following questions.

> Have you ever withdrawn money from an A.T.M ?
> What does A.T.M stand for ?
> Explain what you need to do to get money from an A.T.M.
> Whenever you travel, do you use traveler's checks or credit cards ?
> In Japan, what time do banks close ?
> Can you pay with credits cards at your local supermarket ?
> What about checkbooks? Do you use them for shopping ?

Exercises

A. Choose the correct answer.

1. George is a very good friend of.................
      a. I   b. my   c. me   d. mine

2. New York looks different ....what I thought.
      a. by   b. of   c. from   d. that

3. I have three ....dollars in my current account.
      a. thousand   b. thousand of   c. thousands   d. thousands of

4. We made it on time to the bank. ....we are !
      a. So much luck.   b. What luck   c. Such luck   d. How lucky

5. We'll take either the train............the bus.
      a. whether   b. either   c. or   d. and

B. Translate the following sentences.

1. What is the rate of exchange for the dollar today ?

   ....

2. I can lend you a hundred dollars, if you promise to pay me back next week.

   ....

3. I don't really like to borrow money from people. But, I have no other choice. I have got to buy that lovely dress. It's on sale.

   ....

4. Kazuhiro, don't change your money here. The exchange rate is poor.

   ....

5. You spend too much money. You should save it.

   ....

6. You're right. But, I don't have a savings account.

   ....

7. Is it possible to transfer money to Japan from this bank ?

   ....

Part 2: American VS British English

US	GB
check	cheque
traveler	traveller
license	licence
driver's license	driving licence
We're cutting it a bit close.	We are cutting it a bit fine.
	We are playing it a bit close.

GRAMMAR

The use of **Should, Ought to, Shouldn't**

Examples: - You **should** / **ought to** run to make it on time to work.

- You **should not (shouldn't)** drink that much.

Rules: 1. **Should** and **ought to** are modal auxiliaries. They do not take third person S.

2. Use **should** or **ought to**, to give someone advice, and **shouldn't** to tell someone, something is not a good idea.

The use of **Should** VS **Must, Mustn't** and **Have (got) to**

Examples: - You **should** leave now or you'll be late for work.

- You **must** finish your work before you leave.

- You **mustn't** smoke here.

- I'm sorry. I **have to** go.

Rules: 1. Use **should** to give advice, **must or have to**, to express an obligation or to show that someone is not free to act as he / she would like to, and **mustn't** to show that something is prohibited or not permitted.

2. **Must** can only be used in the present tense. When used in the past, **had to** is used. Ex: I **had to** finish my work.

3. Use **must** to show how certain you are about something.

ENGLISH For DAILY
COMMUNICATION

YOUR TURN 1

Complete the following sentences with: *should, ought to, shouldn't, must, mustn't, have to (or haven't), have got to (haven't got to).*

1. Do you really.....................to go ?
2. I ....go to work tomorrow. (Not an obligation)
3. You ....have warned me.
4. I'm sick. I.....................see the doctor at once.
5. If you want to be paid more, you ....work harder.
6. - ....I invite John to our party ?
   - I don't think you........................ He is such a bad boy.
7. She drives a beautiful car. It..........................be Japanese.
8. She writes to him every day. She.....................love him.

The use of **Could, May, Might, Must**

Modals of probability and possibility

Rules: 1. Use *could, may, might* and ***must*** to tell or show how certain you are or not about a given situation.

Examples:
Bob has such great muscles !

a. He **could** be working out at the gym.
b. He **may** be working out at the gym.
c. He **might** be working out at the gym.
d. He **must** be working out at the gym.

    2. Use *could, might,* or *may* to show that you are not very certain, and must to show that you are almost certain that, this is true.

62 Unit 7

YOUR TURN 2

Study the use of *could, may, might,* and *must* above, then create a situation where you can use them. You can work with a partner.

....

....

....

....

....

Exercises

Choose the correct answer to complete the following sentences. Discuss your choice.

1. The baby looks sick. I think he ....caught a cold.
   a. may have been   b. may have   c. maybe

2. A: My son got a job at the Tokyo Stock Exchange
   B: You ....be very proud of him.
   a. might   b. could   c. must

3. A: Is Bob coming to our party tonight ?
   B: No, he ....working late.
   a. will   b. must   c. is   d. might

4. A: Our friend Liang is giving a violin recital at the Opera of London, this evening.
   B: Oh really, that's great. He ....become very good then.
   a. must   b. must have   c. might have been

5. A: Martha passed her mathematics test.
   B: She.................... She never studies.
   a. could not   b. might not have   c. couldn't have d. must not have

ENGLISH For DAILY
COMMUNICATION

Part 3
Reading: Culture and Civilization

——The United Kingdom: The Houses of Parliament——
Address: Parliament Square SW1; tube: Westminster

The Houses of Parliament are located in the Palace of Westminster, next to the River Thames, in London. It is composed of the House of the Monarch, the House of Commons and the House of Lords.

The House of Commons is the place where Members of Parliament (MPs) sit in session. It is a national assembly of 659 MPs, each one of them elected by local residents to represent a geographical part of the country, called a constituency, in the parliament. In the United Kingdom, everyone aged 18 and over has the right to vote for a local Member of Parliament.

In the House of Commons, government members sit to the right of the Speaker who controls the proceedings and Opposition members to the left.

The House of Lords has about 700 Members, most of them appointed for life by the Prime Minister. This is where Her Majesty the Queen comes to open Parliament each November.

——————Parliament and Government——————

Parliament's job is to approve new laws before they come into force as acts of parliament. It also keeps a check on the work of government on behalf of citizens through investigative select committees and by asking ministers questions. Whereas the government's job is to run the country.

After each national election, the leader of the political party with the most MPs in the House of Commons is asked by the Queen to become Prime Minister and to form the government that will manage the country.

Source: Adapted from *aboutbritain.com*

Unit 8

I've got a scratchy throat.
I might be coming down with a cold.

Part 1: Conversation

—————————— At the Drugstore ——————————

Mrs. R: Mrs. Robert   P: pharmacist

P : Hi. Can I help you ?

Mrs. R : Yes, please. Could you recommend something for my husband, he has a terrible cold. I couldn't drag him to the drugstore.

P : Could you describe his symptoms ?

Mrs. R : He seems to have a headache, and a sore throat. He's also been coughing since last night, and his body aches all over.

P : Well, it certainly sounds like flu. Didn't he get his flu vaccine this year ?

Mrs. R : I doubt it, otherwise he would have told me.

P : Right. I suggest a box of these "Anti-cold" tablets, with some cough drops.

Mrs. R : Will the tablets make him drowsy ?

P : A little bit, but he'd better not drive while taking them.

Mrs. R : Are these drugs good ?

P : Yes, they should work. However, if he is not back on his feet in a couple of days, I would suggest he sees a doctor. Would you like anything else ?

Mrs. R : No, that's it. How much will that be ?

P : Exactly $15. Here you are.

Mrs. R : Thank you very much.

P : It's my pleasure.

Watch out ! There are cops.

Questions

1. Write a summary of the conversation above in a few lines. (no longer than six lines)

2. Answer the following questions.

   Have you ever had a sore throat ?
   What did you do ?
   How many times have you been sick in the last few months ?
   What did you have ?
   What did you take for it ?
   What would you advise to someone who has these common health complaints :

   a fever ?
   a cough ?
   the flu ?
   a toothache ?
   a backache ?
   sore muscles ?
   a headache ?
   a burn ?

Exercises

A. Choose the correct answer.

   1. My father is suffering ....back pain.
      a. at   b. in   c. on   d. from

   2. I caught a cold yesterday ....the air-conditioning.
      a. by   b. at   c. from   d. on

   3. John, what are the pills you've been taking ....?
      a. calling   b. to be called   c. called   d. being called

4. I ....money left to pay for insurance.
      a. have any   b. haven't got no   c. haven't got any   d. have got any

5. At the hospital, we didn't know...............he was complaining about.
      a. why   b. that   c. what   d. whether

6. I haven't seen Linda for awhile. She may ....ill.
      a. being   b. to be   c. that she is   d. be

B. Translate the following sentences.

1. My daughter didn't feel well last night. I had to call an ambulance to take her to the hospital.

    ....

2. Hardly had we arrived at the hospital than she started to vomit.

    ....

3. Be careful! Your blood pressure is too high.

    ....

4. Paul hurt himself during a football match yesterday. He had to get an X-ray to make sure he did not have a sprain or a fracture.

    ....

    ....

5. A: My tooth is killing me ! I don't know what's wrong with it.

    ....

    B: It can be serious. You should see the dentist immediately.

    ....

    A: Thanks for your advice. I'll do just that.

    ....

6. My eyes hurt, I need some eye drops.

....

7. Watch your diet Linda. You tend to gain weight easily.

....

8. Take two of these tablets every two hours, but not more than four per day.

....

Part 2: American VS British English

US	GB
drugstore	chemist's
pharmacist, druggist	chemist
diarrhea	diarrhoea
old home remedies	old wives' cures

GRAMMAR

The use of **Much, many, a lot**

Examples:
- I haven't got **much** time.
- There were **many** people at my party.
- He has **a lot of** (or plenty or a great deal of) money.

Rules: 1. Use *much* with non count nouns to talk about a large number.
2. Use *many* only with count nouns to talk about a large number
3. *Much* and *many* are usually used in negative statements or in questions.
4. Use *a lot of* or *lots of* or *a great deal of* or *plenty of* with very large numbers or amounts, and with either count or non count nouns.

YOUR TURN 1

Complete the following sentences using *many*, *much* or *a lot (of)* when possible.

1. A: Hi Jim, what's up ?
   B: Not ....
2. My sister doesn't read.................books but she reads.....................
   comics.
3. There isn't ....room in my new car.
4. You should drink ....water, it's good for your health.
5. There are now................foreigners living in Japan.
6. I have got ....English and American friends.
7. Have you got.................pets ?
8. A: I've got too ....CDs. Take as................as you like.
   B: Thank you very.................
9. A: Have you traveled to ....countries ?
   B: Not ....

YOUR TURN 2

Give the opposite of the following words.

certain.................	healthy.................	interesting........................
to trust...............	to hope.................	modern.............................
full.....................	satisfied...............	dead..............................
ordinary.....................	obedient.................	kind...............................
drunk.....................	old..........................	dry..............................
difficult...................	heavy...................	poor.............................
rough.....................	happy...................	weak............................

YOUR TURN 3

What is a young......

cat ?.....................	dog ?.....................	cow ?........................
horse ?.................	sheep ?.................	duck ?.......................
hen ?.....................	swan ?.................	goose ?......................

Part 3
Reading: Culture and Civilization

—The Political system: The Constitution of the U.S.A—

Part 1

The constitution of the United States was shaped and signed at the convention of 1787, in Philadelphia by representatives of the 13 original States. It is based on **four principles**:

1. Federalism
One country, the United States of America; a Confederation of 50 States, each retaining *"its sovereignty, freedom and independence and every power which is not expressly delegated to the United States..."(1)*

2. Separation of Powers
Executive Power: is in the hands of one President (Chief Executive); *Legislative* Power: bicameral (two Houses: The Senate and the House of Representatives) Independent *Judiciary* Power: the 9 Federal Judges who compose the Supreme court are appointed for life by the President with the consent of the Senate (a formula which provides for both continuity and poise in the administration of justice).

3. Checks and Balances
- Between the Executive and Legislative: the President can *veto* a Bill, but Congress can *override* the veto; Congress cannot force the President to act and the latter cannot stop a law, but a system of compromises has developed, allowing them to counterbalance each other;
- Between the Federal and State Governments (1) the power relationship between them is not always clear, but there is a modern tendency towards federal/state co-operation.

4. Judiciary review.

The courts – with the Supreme Court having the final say – can declare an act of the Congress unconstitutional. They can do the same with a State or Federal Law. They also act as arbiters in disputes between private citizens and the U.S.A.

(1) In each State:
  - Executive, a Governor, elected by direct vote (except in Mississippi);
  - Legislative, two Houses (except in Nebraska, only one);
  - Judiciary, Justices of the Peace (J.P's); County Courts and a Supreme State Court.

Part 2

The Federal Government

In the United States, the political power is shared between the Congress (Legislative Power) and the President (Executive Power).

Legislative Power is retained by the Congress, and is shared between *The Senate* and *The House of Representatives.*

1. *The Senate* counts 100 members, 2 for each state, elected for six years and renewed by thirds every two years.
2. *The House of Representatives* counts 435 members elected for 2 years. The number for each state depends on the population (about 400 000 inhabitants for one seat).
   - The Congress declares war;
   - The Senate ratifies Treaties;
   - A Bill (law) must pass both houses;
   - Presidential Veto can be overridden by a 2/3 majority in both Houses;
   - The House of Representatives initiates Tax Bills; the Senate may amend or reject them;
   - The Senate must agree to nominations of high officials;
   - The Congress can impeach the President by a 2/3 majority.

Executive Power lies with The President who is elected for 4 years. He or She can be re – elected only once. The President is assisted by a Vice–President and a Cabinet with Secretaries (Heads of Departments) (2). :

- The President is the Commander in Chief of the Armed Forces. He or She can deploy them wherever he or she thinks fit;
- He or She can Initiate Foreign Policy;
- Signs the Bills, issues Executive orders to put them into effect;
- Can also veto a Bill.
- Recommends a yearly legislature address ("on the State of the Union") to the Congress and prepares the National Budget.
- Nominates upper Government Officials;
- Cannot dissolve Congress.

(2) State Department (Foreign Affairs), Treasury, Defense, Justice, Interior, Agriculture, Labor, Commerce, Health – Education – Welfare, Housing and Urban Development, and Transportation.

Adapted From *The U.S.A in your Pocket*, D. ENGLE

What a view !

Have you ever visited the Statue of Liberty ?

Unit 9

Let's go out to the mall for a movie.

Part 1: Conversation

──────── Going to the Movies ────────

K: Kevin   S: Susan

S : Kevin, what time do you think you'll be back from work this evening ?

K : I should be back by 6. Is there anything special you want to do ?

S : Not really, but I thought you and I could go to the movies tonight. That would allow you to get your mind off your work and I need to get out of the house. How about it ?

K : Yeah ! That's a great idea. What's playing ? Is it one of your favorite horror movies ?

S : Not this time. What about The Passion of The Christ ? Everyone is talking about it ?

K : I'd love to. We'll have to go downtown. What time is the show ?

S : Let me check the paper's entertainment section. It's 10:00.

K : That gives us plenty of time to have dinner before the show, right ?

S : Right. What do you want to eat ?

K : I feel like eating Japanese. How about Sushi ?

S : Raw fish again ? Don't you remember how sick I was last time we ate at a Sushi bar ? What about Tempura ?

K : A bit oily but that's fine with me, as long as it's Japanese.

Questions ──────────────────────────────

1. Write a summary of the conversation above. (no longer than six lines)

2. Answer the following questions.

Do you like movies ?

How many times a month do you go to the movie theater ?

What is the last movie that you saw ?

When and where did you see it ?

Who was in it ?

What was it about ?

Did you enjoy it ? Why ?

Exercises

A. Choose the correct answer.

1. What time ....the film begin ?
    a. did   b. do   c. does   d. is

2. That film sells out wherever it is..............
    a. showing   b. show   c. showed   d. shown

3. I won't have you ....that sort of thing about Mel Gibson. He is a great actor.
    a. say   b. to saying   c. said   d. to say

4. A: Come over for dinner this week-end !
   B: I'd like..............
    a. I did   b. to   c. it   d. so

5. Now let me be clearly................
    a. understood   b. understanding   c. understand
    d. to understand

B. Translate the following sentences.

1. I like cartoons better than anything else.

....

2. "The Last Samurai" sold $100,000,000 in tickets in the first week.

....

3. Dicaprio won an Oscar for his role in Titanic.

....

4. In Star Wars, the special effects are mind-boggling.

....

5. I read the script, it is ludicrous.

....

6. My mom likes detective films. She watches them on TV every week.

....

7. This movie has got a great cast.

....

8. I'd like to see the undubbed version.

....

Part 2: American VS British English

US	GB
the movies	the pictures; the cinema
a movie	a picture; a film
downtown	into town
the movie theater	the cinema
show	performance

GRAMMAR

Part 1

The use of **a few, a little, few, little**

Examples:
1. **a few minutes** later
2. **a little** later
3. **a few** friends
4. I have **little** money
5. "Do you speak Japanese ?" "**A little**"

Rules: *A few* and *a little* have similar meanings. However, use *a few* with count nouns and *a little* with non count nouns.

Use *few* with count nouns and *little* with non count nouns. They have a negative meaning. They mean *almost none*.

YOUR TURN 1

A. Complete the following sentences with a few or a little, few or little.

1. In England, the Queen has....................power.
2. ....people came to his party.
3. "Was he disappointed ?" "....................."
4. I've been to London ....times.
5. A: "How are you feeling today ?"
   B: ".................better thanks.
6. Sir, I've got ....questions to ask you about today's lesson.
7. Excuse me, could I have ....water for my kid ?

Part 2

Comparatives and Superlatives

1. with short adjectives (one syllable)

	Comparative	Superlative
old	old**er than**	**the** old**est**
fast	fast**er than**	**the** fast**est**
easy	easi**er than**	**the** easi**est**

2. Irregular

good	**better**	**the best**
bad	**worse**	**the worst**
far	**further / farther**	**the furthest / farthest**

3. With long adjectives (two or more syllable)

difficult	**more difficult than**	**the most difficult**
sensitive	**more sensitive than**	**the most sensitive**

4. With much / many, little and few

much / many	**more**	**the most**
little	**less**	**the least**
few	**fewer**	**the fewest**

5. With as _____ as / not as _____ as

as old **as**	**as** fast **as**
not as beautiful **as**	**not as** quick **as**

6. With more and more; less and less

more and more beautiful
less and less patient

Mme Tussauds (London)

YOUR TURN 2

A. Complete the following sentences with a comparative or superlative.

1. English is ....maths. (easy)
2. Summer is ....season of the year. (hot)
3. Football is ....baseball. (interesting)
4. I think education is ....thing in life. (important)
5. ....planet from the sun is called Pluto. (far)

B. Complete the following sentences with better, best, worse, or worst.

1. Yesterday, the New York Yankees played ....than expected.
2. Ron's grade in the last maths test was even ....than in the previous one.
3. Michael Jordan's ....performance with the Chicago Bulls was against the L.A. Lakers.
4. Last summer humidity in Japan was the...............I have ever experienced.
5. My ....friend is going to the U.S.A next month to study English for one year.
6. "Not even a hundred at bowling ? Come on Jerry, you can do ....than that. Don't tell me that was your..............shot !"

C. Complete the following sentences with less, least, fewer.

1. I need at ....two more hours to complete this work.
2. It's the ....interesting story I have ever heard.
3. I earn ....money than my father does.
4. There are ....exploited children in Nike factories now around the world than there used to be.
5. The cost of living in England is ....expensive than in Japan.

YOUR TURN 3

Explain the following idioms:

1. To have stage fright.

....

2. A preview of a film.

....

3. A film premiere.

....

4. A first night.

....

5. To go back-stage.

....

6. A matinee performance.

....

7. A dress rehearsal.

....

Part 3
Reading: Culture and Civilization

————————The USA: The Dream Factory————————

Hollywood, the American film city, a suburb of Los Angeles, was founded in 1912, when a number of independent producers headed west from New York. By 1913, Hollywood was established as the film makers' factory and continues to be one to this day.

"Hollywood's own history resembles the plot of a classic Hollywood crime film. Rival gangs decide to make an arrangement and carve up the territory between them. For awhile Mr. Big and Mr. Bad honor this agreement...bringing in the police and the politicians. Then, however, something goes wrong. Competition starts up again. Mr. Big and Mr. Bad are both gunned down by their former partners' hired hands..."

Jeremy Tunstall

The movie industry

Sound came to motion pictures only months before the Great Depression enveloped America. The concentration of capital necessary for this conversion, coupled with the financial crisis which prevailed then, forced the major companies to turn to the eastern banking firms. In this manner, the banks expanded their holdings and greatly increased their influence in the motion picture industry. All of the major movie companies underwent extensive financial reorganization, which eventually led to domination of the major studios by their sources of financing.

The ultimate product of this reorganization was a hierarchy of eight major companies:

• The "Big Five" – the companies which controlled production, distribution and exhibition – were MGM, Paramount, RKO, Twentieth Century-Fox, and Warner Brothers.

• The "little Three" were Columbia, United Artists and Universal.

Together, the eight controlled 95 percent of the films shown during this period in the United States.

Robert Stanley. *The Celluloid Empire*

How long does it take to get to Honolulu from LA ?

Unit 10

We could rent a car and...

Part 1: Conversation

────────── Renting a Car ──────────

A: Agent   C: Customer

A : Hello ! How can I help you ?

C : Yes, I'd like to rent a car. What kind of car do you have ?

A : It depends on what you have in mind.

C : Well, my friend and I are from Japan. What we'd like to do is get a car here in London, drive to Birmingham, then on to Liverpool to watch the match Liverpool versus Manchester. Is it possible to drop it off there ?

A : I'm afraid that won't be possible because we don't have an office in Liverpool.

C : That's a pity ! I thought we could fly to Dublin from there. In that case, what would you suggest ?

A : You could leave the car in Manchester where we do have an office.

C : All right. Would you please tell me what the rates are ? We'd like to keep the car for five days.

A : Take a look at this brochure. There are daily and weekly rates for each type of car. However, at this moment we've only got type E available. It is the 4WD Range Rover parked over there. Everything else is already booked.

C : My goodness, type E is the most expensive one.

A : Yes, but it has the air-conditioning, a little fridge, the phone, a great stereo system with a CD changer.

C : At this price we might just as well take the train, or even fly.

A : I see what you mean. But you won't be charged for not returning the car here, and at least you'll get to see the country.

C: It's a real bargain then! We'll take it for a week.

Questions

1. Write a summary of the conversation above in a few lines. (no longer than six lines).

2. Answer the following questions.

   Do you have a driver's license ?
   How long did it take you to get it ?
   How often do you drive ?
   What is your favorite car ? Why ?
   Have you ever rented a car ?
   What do you need to be able to rent a car in Japan ? (If you don't know, please look for that information).

Exercises

A. Choose the correct answer.

1. In my car trunk, there is ....of room for the luggage.
   a. many   b. enough   c. plenty   d. some

2. ....miles per day do you plan to do ?
   a. How much   b. How long   c. How often   d. How many

3. Accidents on this road have been ....numerous this year.
   a. far many   b. a few less   c. far much   d. far less

4. I have exactly ....same car as yours.
   a. some   b. a   c. one   d. the

5. Toyota Motors started to produce this model.................1980.
   a. in the early   b. as early as   c. as soon as   d. soon as

6. Nissan and Toyota cannot merge because there are many differences between ....companies.

    a. either   b. the two   c. the both   d. both

B. Translate the following sentences.

1. Car rentals can be found in all airports.

    ....

2. What kind of gas does this vehicle take ?

    ....

3. This car has automatic transmission.

    ....

4. Sorry to have kept you waiting.

    ....

5. It's cheaper to rent a car on a weekly basis.

    ....

6. A: Where is the ignition key ?

    ....

    B: It's in the dashboard.

    ....

Part 2: American VS British English

US	GB
hood	bonnet
compact	small car
dashboard	dash board
exhaust	exhaust pipe
fender	wing
gas tank	petrol tank
gear shift lever	gear lever
license plate	number plate
muffler	silencer
parking lot	car park
pedestrian crossing	zebra crossing
pick up	open lorry
rest area	lay-by
sedan	saloon car
spark plug	sparking plug
station wagon	estate car
tail lights	rearlights
tire	tyre
traffic circle	roundabout
trailer	caravan
truck	lorry
trunk	boot
to yield right of way	to give way
windshield	windscreen
xing	crossing

GRAMMAR

Part 1

The use of **Any** and **Some**

Examples:
- Have you got *any* stamps ?
- I haven't *any* money
- I'd like *some* tea, please.

Rules: 1. Use *any* with interrogative or negative sentences.
2. Use *some* with affirmative sentences.

YOUR TURN 1

Complete the following sentences with *some* or *any*.

1. There is ....money in the box. – is it yours ?
2. Would she like ....wine ?
3. They haven't got ....dogs or cats.
4. A: Are there ....Japanese people living in Liverpool ?
   B: Yes, I think there are...................
5. We've hardly got................milk in the fridge.

Part 2

The use of **somebody, anything, anywhere, everywhere, everything, no-one / nobody, somewhere**

YOUR TURN 2

Complete the following sentences with *somebody, anything, anywhere, everything, or no-one / nobody, everywhere, somewhere, anybody.*

1. Lisa is such a sweet girl. I think ....hates her.
2. I have seen you ....
3. A: Did ....called when I was away ?

   B: Yes, ...did, but I forgot to write down his name. I'm sorry about that.
4. Is there ....at the club ?
5. There is ....else, but the bartender.
6. I don't know where to start looking for the dog. It can be ....
7. ....I go, I hear people talking about you. What have you done ?
8. Have you taken ....for your headache ?
9. The car is empty.......................is gone. ....has stolen our luggage. We must report to the police.
10. A: Do you know where the morning paper is, Bob ?

    B: I think I saw it.........................in the kitchen.
11. I heard Linda now lives.........................near Central Park in New York.

YOUR TURN 3

Give the opposite of the following words.

economical.....................

increase..........................

present...........................

joy......................

underpaid..........................

to add..........................

well........................

to hate...............................

industrious......................

to remember....................

anxious..............................

strength.........................

to fail.......................

exact...............................

foolish............................

Part 3
Reading: Culture and Civilization

—————— Higher Education in the U.K. ——————

Someone is said to be highly educated when he or she has got a degree given at a university.

In the UK, there are said to be 88 universities, which includes one private university (Buckingham) and the one that provides distance learning (the Open University).

There were only six universities until the 19th century, Oxford, Cambridge, and the four ancient Scottish universities – St Andrews, Glasgow, Aberdeen and Edinburgh. London University was founded in 1836. It was then the first new university, and was organized in colleges following the pattern of Oxford and Cambridge.

London University is now the largest university in the UK with over 30 colleges scattered all over London and Counties.

Universities in the UK are ranked according to a set of criteria that involves publishing, research, graduate and undergraduate courses. They all receive funding that depends on their ranking.

The Government is encouraging universities to cooperate closely with industry on research. Today, there are more than 50 science parks set up by higher education institutions together with industrial scientists and technologists where the development and commercial application of advanced technology are promoted. However, there are no Arts Parks.

Source: adapted from www.eng.umu.se/education

Unit 11

On the wide open road it's easy to forget the speed limit.

New Jersey viewed from the air.

Part 1: Conversation

─────────── **An Encounter with the Police** ───────────

K: Ken   H: Harry   O: Police Officer

K : Harry, I'd like to thank you for inviting me here to South Dakota

H : It's my pleasure, Ken.

K : I'm so excited because this is the first time I'm going to visit Mount Rushmore. I can also tell you that, driving on this highway is a lot of fun.

H : Do you drive a lot in Japan ?

K : Yes, I do but most of the time, you get stuck in traffic jams.

H : I see what you mean. By the way, there's a car with a flashing red light following us and it doesn't look like an ambulance to me.

K : Is it the police ?

H : I'm afraid, yes.

K : Damn. What should I do ?

H : You'd better pull over. The policeman is signaling to you to do that. Calm down and roll down your window.

O : Hi! Do you know what the speed limit is on this highway ?

K : I think it is 70 m.p.h.

O : You're right. So, how fast were you driving before I stopped you.

K : I believe I was doing 65 or so.

O : Are you kidding me ? You were doing at least 100 when I spotted you.

K : I'm terribly sorry, Officer. I wasn't aware that I was driving that fast.

O : Let me see you driver's license and registration papers ?

K : Here's my license.

O : It's not even in English ! You're driving without a valid license and speeding on top of it. You'll have to come with me to the precinct. Where's the registration ?

K : Officer, this is a rented car...

O : I see. Where are you from ?

K : I'm from Tokyo, Japan.

O : Listen, I'll let you off this time, but don't get caught again.

K : Gee, that was a very close call. If he had taken me to the station, I would have been in trouble.

H : You did very well, Ken.

Questions

1. Write a summary of the conversation above in a few lines. (no longer than six lines)

2. Answer the following questions.

   Have you ever got a speeding ticket ?
   In Japan, what is the speed limit on the highway ? In the city ?
   Have you ever got a parking ticket ? How much was the fine ?
   Are there many traffic accidents in Japan ? (please find out how many people die from traffic accidents and what are the main causes of accidents ?
   Have you ever been involved in or witnessed a traffic accident ?
   Tell us what happened ?
   According to you, what is a good driver and what is a bad driver ?

Exercises

A. Choose the correct answer.

   1. This man is a very bad drive. He went ....a red light
         a. on   b. through   c. by   d. at

   2. Someone is robbing the bank. I have to report it.........the police.
         a. at   b. in   c. to   d. by

   3. As a witness, you will be called.........to court.
         a. in   b. on   c. at   d. for

4. Yesterday, a motorcyclist was killed ....the accident.

      a. by   b. at   c. into   d. in

5. A: Excuse me, where can I find the police station near here ?

   B: Turn...............at the lights, there's one just nearby. You can't miss it.

      a. right   b. on right   c. to right   d. by right

B. Translate the following sentences.

1. A vision test is given to all applicants for the learner's permit.

   ....

2. My little sister was severely injured by a hit and run driver.

   ....

3. In the USA, the speed limit varies from state to state.

   ....

4. Officer, my driver's licence and registration papers were stolen.

   ....

Part 2: American VS British English

US	GB
gee	gosh
highway	motorway
precinct	police station
run in	encounter
to pass	to overtake
signaling	signalling

GRAMMAR

THE CONDITIONAL TENSE

Part 1

1. Present conditional

Examples:
- She **would come**
- He **would not know**
- I **would go**
- **I'd be angry**
- It **wouldn't be** nice

Rules: Form the conditional with **"would + the infinitive of the verb without to"**

2. The conditional with an "if" clause

Examples:
- **If you invite** me to the restaurant, I **will accept** with pleasure.
- **If you told** me the truth, it **would be** easier to help you.

3. Past and past perfect conditional

Examples:
- He **would have spoken**
- She **wouldn't have gone**
- **If you invited** me to the restaurant, I **would accept** with pleasure
- **If you had invited** me to the restaurant, I **would have accepted** with pleasure
- If I **had known**, I **would have done** something

Rules: Form the conditional in the past with **"would + have + past participle"**

YOUR TURN 1

Complete the following sentences: with will or would.

1. I ....buy a car if I could afford it.
2. When it's cooler, I ....go running.
3. I ....learn the piano if I had enough time.
4. If it was cooler, I ....go running.
5. I ....learn the piano next year if I have enough time.

YOUR TURN 2

Complete the following sentences with the correct form of the verb.

1. If I ....enough money I would take you to the restaurant. (to have)
2. If you had not left earlier, you ....the new English teacher. (to meet)
3. I.................smoking if I had more will-power. (to quit)
4. What.............you..............if you were rich ? (to do)
5. I won't go out if it .... (to rain)

YOUR TURN 3

Complete the following sentences.

1. If I were you...
2. I should never have gone if......................................
3. You could easily finish this job if............................
4. If you help me ....
5. If you work hard...

Part 2

1. Factual conditionals with "if" clause

Examples:

- If you put butter into a hot pan, it melts.
- If you pour water into a fire, it extinguishes the fire.
- If you leave milk in the sun, it turns sour.

Rules: Use factual conditionals to talk about things that you expect to happen, in certain situations.

2. Hypothetical conditionals with *"would", "might", "may" and "will"*

- If I were you, **I would** be very angry.
- If I found myself swimming in the middle of the ocean surrounded by sharks, **I might** try to swim faster to the shore.
- If I hadn't woken up late, I **may have** made it on time for the exam.
- If the weather is fine tomorrow, I **will** go to the beach.

Rules: Use **would** to express the most probable result; **might** or **may** to show that you are not certain of the result, although it is likely or possible to happen; and **will** to show that your are certain of the result.

YOUR TURN 4

Make a list of ten flowers and ten vegetables.

Flowers	Vegetables
1.	....
2.	....
3.	....
4.	....
5.	....
6.	....

7. ....

8. ....

9. ....

10. ....

Part 3
Reading: Culture and Civilization

The Police in the USA

There is no national police corps in the United States. Police departments are organized and run at city or community level, and the position of chief of police is an elected one.

The nature of law enforcement differs from one state to another. However, standards are similar concerning eligibility for appointment, training, duties, promotions and salaries.

The FBI (Federal Bureau of Investigation created in 1908) only investigates violations of Federal laws. Its MOTTO: *"Fidelity, Bravery, and Integrity"*

The mission of the FBI is to protect and defend the United States against terrorist and foreign intelligence threats, to uphold and enforce the criminal laws of the United States, and to provide leadership and criminal justice services to federal, state, municipal, and international agencies and partners.

Source: Adapted from *http://www.fbi.gov*

Unit 12

What kind of gas does this car take ?

Part 1: Conversation

———————— At the Service Station ————————

C: Customer   A: Attendant

A : Hi ! How can I help you ?

C : I'd like some gas please.

A : What kind of gas do you want ?

C : The problem is that I don't really know. You see, this is a rented car and it's the first time I'm getting gas. What kind of gas do you think it may take ?

A : We have hi-test, unleaded and regular. The car you're driving takes only unleaded. Do you want me to fill it up ?

C : Yes, please.

A : How about the oil ?

C : I thought I had to see a mechanic for that, but if you can check it that would be great. Can you check the water and tires as well ?

A : Certainly.

C : Do you have toilets here ?

A : Yes, right over there.

C : Did you take care of the oil and water ?

A : Yes, it took a quart of oil and some water, but the tires were all right. That will be $28.

C : Here you are.

A : Here's your change.

C : One more thing. Is there a restaurant nearby ? I've been on the road for nearly four hours, and I'm really starving.

A : Turn at the second set of lights on your left. There you'll see a sign for Burger King. Follow the sign to Burger King. You can't miss it.

C : Thanks ever so much.

Questions

1. Write a summary of the conversation above in a few lines. (no more than six lines)

2. Answer the following questions.

What kind of gas does your car take ? (yours or your family's)
What is the price of gas now in Japan ?
Why does the price of gas sometimes go up ?
Name five companies that sell gas in Japan ? Which one do you prefer ? Why ?

Exercises

A. Choose the correct answer.

1. Officer, I didn't do anything wrong. What offence am I guilty ....
   a. with   b. in   c. for   d. of

2. ...., the officer exclaimed.
   a. "What this man is funny !"   b. "How funny this man is !"
   c. "Such funny this man is !"   d. "How this man is funny !"

3. Why did you drive through the red light ? It's high time you...................
   a. will answer   b. have answered   c. answer   d. answered

4. I'll let you off this time but don't do that again. "...............you are !"
   a. So much luck   b. What luck   c. Such luck   d. How lucky

5. From now on, I'll take either the train...............the bus.
   a. whether   b. or   c. either   d. and

B. Translate the following sentences.

1. Don't forget to turn your headlights on at dusk.

   ....

2. Would you check the tire pressure please ?

   ....

3. I had a flat and I had to be towed.

   ....

4. I'd better check the spare tire in the trunk.

   ....

5. Yield the right of way.

   ....

6. I have got two parking tickets and I was fined for speeding.

   ....

Part 2: American VS British English

US	GB
back-up lights	reversing lights
crosswalk	pedestrian crossing
filling station	petrol station
gas	petrol
tire	tyre
thru	through
men's room	gents (gentlemen)
windshield	windscreen

GRAMMAR

Imperatives

Examples:
1.   **Stay** here.   **Go** out.   **Stop** talking.

Rules: An imperative is formed with the infinitive of the verb without to
You can also use an imperative to give advice. However, in some
cases it would be better to use **should / shouldn't / ought to**.

2. Imperative negative

Examples:
    Don't go.   **Don't forget** to write.

Rules: Use **_don't_** to form an imperative negative

YOUR TURN 1

Give advice.
● What would you tell someone with:

A cough ?...
The flu ?...
Insomnia ?...
A toothache ?...
A headache ?..
Stress ?..

● What would you say:

To a child who cries ?...
To someone who is always drunk ?...............................
To someone who is overweight ?.....................................

To a lazy boy ?...

To someone who drives to fast ?...

To someone who smokes too much ?.......................................

To someone who lacks courage ?...

YOUR TURN 2

Explain the following idioms:

1. To give someone a lift.
2. To hitch-hike.
3. A short cut.
4. The rush hour.
5. A speed limit.
6. Traffic lights.
7. Traffic lanes.
8. Parking meters
9. To take a driving test.
10. To pour oil on troubled waters
11. No overtaking.
12. To skate on thin ice.
13. A patrol car.
14. A hit and run driver.
15. A by-pass.

YOUR TURN 3

Make sentences with the following words.

1. efficient...
2. effective...
3. discover...
4. invent...
5. elder...

6. older..

7. remind..

8. remember...

9. thankful..

10. grateful...

11. last...

12. latest..

13. lay..

14. lie...

YOUR TURN 4

Give the opposite of the following words.

human	superior	neat ....
freedom	fortunate	advantage ....
passive	profound	doubt ....
luxury	foolish	majority ....
order	similarity	complete ....
expansion	agreement	equality ....
violence	arrival	exterior ....

I'll have a "Big Mac" burger-hold the mustard.
Sorry, I mean "Whopper".

Part 3
Reading: Culture and Civilization

————— Canada & Ecology : Climate Change —————

Climate change is one of the most significant environmental challenges the world has ever faced. The impacts of climate change on our health, economy, and environment require that some action be taken.

With the ratification of the Kyoto Protocol, the Government of Canada has made climate change a national priority, and works closely with Canadians and the global community to meet this challenge.

Climate change issues are co-managed by the Minister of the Environment and the Minister of Natural Resources. Other federal government departments such as the provincial/territorial Ministers of Energy and Environment, municipalities, as well as scientists, industry, the business community and individual Canadians are also involved.

The Budget committed by the government to climate change action since 2000 is $3.7 billion. This money is invested in infrastructure, technology, science and in regional development in order to achieve the climate change objectives. These objectives are: to reduce greenhouse gas emissions, build more livable cities with a cleaner environment and increase competitiveness.

Source: Adapted from *Environment Canada http://www.ec.gc.ca*

Kids, this old boat was used long ago on the Red River in Manitoba, Canada.

Unit 13

Oh, she's out ?
Could you give her a message please ?

Part 1: Conversation

————————On the phone 1: *Information* ————————

O: Operator   C: Customer

O : AT&T, how can I help you ?

C : Hello, information ?

O : Yes, what city are you calling ?

C : Bethesda, MD. ...Please could you give me the number of a Mr. Johnson, 6790 Montgomery Avenue.

O : Certainly. Just a minute please. What is his first name ?

C : I believe it's Bill.

O : Is that North or South Montgomery Ave ?

C : I wish I knew. Does it really matter ?

O : Well, I've got three Johnsons on Montgomery. Do you have the middle initial ?

C : I'm sorry I don't know. Could you give me the three numbers, if you don't mind ?

O : Sure. 462-8517, 365-8865 and 593-8326

C : Thanks operator. Would you please put the call through for me ?

O : You can dial it direct, quite easily. First the area code, then the number.

C : And what is the area code ? Sorry I don't have a directory ?

O : It's 301.

C : One last question. What time is it now in Maryland ?

O : It's 9 o'clock in the morning.

C : That means we're three hours behind. Thanks once again.

O : You're welcome.

Questions

1. Write a summary of the conversation above in a few lines. (no more than six lines)

2. Answer the following questions.

What number do you need to dial to call for information, the police, and the fire department in Japan ?
What is the area code for Tokyo, Osaka, and Kyoto ?
Where do you live ? What is the area code for that city ?
What are the main phone companies here in Japan ?
Is there any foreign phone company operating in Japan ? Which one ?

On the phone 2: *Telephone messages*

V: A voice   T: Mr. Turner

V : Good morning, Johnson & Johnson Corporation.

T : Hello. May I speak to Mr. Carlson, please?

V : Who is calling ?

T : This is Mr. Turner from New York.

V : I'm sorry. He is not in right now, but he should be back soon. Would you like to leave a message ?

T : Yes, please.

V : Is your name spelt D-O-N-N-A ?

T : No, it's T-U-R-N-E-R.

V : I'm sorry Mr. Turner.

T : Please tell him I will be arriving at Tokyo Narita the day after tomorrow at 1 p.m. local time.

V : Can he call you back ?

T : Yes, my number is 212-464-8617.

V : 212-464-8617. Yes, Mr. Turner. I'll give Mr. Carlson the message.

T : Thank you very much.

V : You're welcome.

Questions

1. Write a summary of the conversation above in a few lines. (no more than six lines)

Exercises

A. Look at the situations below. Ask somebody to pass on these messages.

(1) You would like to invite Ron to your home party. He is not at home and you decide to leave a message.

....

....

....

....

(2) You are to meet with your girl friend or boy friend at 4: 00 p.m. to go to the movies. You're running 10 minutes late. You call but you've got an answering machine saying: "This is Tom Lehman. I can't come to the phone right now, leave a message and I'll call you back."

....

....

....

....

(3) You call for Bob. He is not in. His mother, Mrs. Cashman picks up the phone. You want Bob to return your call as soon as possible.

....

....

....

....

(4) A friend of yours, Susan invited you for dinner. At the very last minute something comes up. You can't make it. You call, but she is not in. Her father Mr. Smith picks up the phone. You decide to leave a message.

....

....

....

....

B. Choose the correct answer.

1. Check your number before................
     a. dialed   b. dialing   c. to dial   d. dial

2. I have got exactly...........same cellular phone as yours.
     a. some   b. a   c. one   d. the

3. "I think the line is busy now. Would you mind...............again later ?"
     a. try   b. to try   c. of trying   d. trying

4. I won't have you ....that kind of nonsense.
     a. say   b. to say   c. to saying   d. said

5. Can you spare me ten minutes ? ....
     a. Yes, I do   b. No, I won't   c. Yes, I can   d. Yes, I can do

6. I'm looking forward to ....soon
     a. be allowed to hear you   b. hearing from you
     c. hear you   d. have to hear you

C. Translate the following sentences.

1. Sorry, the number you're trying to reach is busy at the moment. Try again later.

....

2. Could you please tell me the area code for Washington DC, I don't have a directory ?

....

3. I'd like to place a call to Chicago, IL. 756-2587

....

4. Hold the line please.

....

5. I've been cut off.

....

6. I'd like to make a collect call to Japan.

....

7. Who is calling please ?

....

8. You've got the wrong number.

....

9. Hang on please ! I'll get him for you.

....

10. Can you put me through to extension 101 please ?

....

Part 2: American VS British English

US	GB
area code	local code, STD code
	STD (Subscriber Trunk Dialling)
information	directory inquiries
dial tone	dialling tone
long distance call	trunk call
phone booth	phone box
the line is busy	the line is engaged
dialed/dialing	dialled/dialling

GRAMMAR

The use of **Say** and **Tell**

Examples:
- **Say** what you want.
- **Say** hello to John.
- **Say** your name to me.
- **Tell me** your name.
- **Tell her** what you want.
- **Tell us** the story.
- He **said** that he was fine.
- He **told me** that he was fine.

Rules: You *say* something *to* somebody, but you *tell* somebody something.

YOUR TURN 1

Complete the following sentences using say or tell.

1. She is ....everybody how bad her husband is.
2. Michael Jackson is...............to be the king of pop music.

3. A: What did you ....to your girl friend ?

   B: I.................her she was the most beautiful girl in the world.

   A: Did you really..............that to her ?

   B: Of course I did.

   A: And what did she ....then ?

   B: She ....she didn't believe me at all.

4. Mrs. Grant likes to................children stories.

5. When I was younger, my mom used to ....me not to speak to strangers on my way to school.

6. It's not good to..............a lie.

7. Why do you always.................such bad things to people ? It hurts, you know.

8. I ....I wouldn't do that again.

YOUR TURN 2

Give the opposite of the following words.

attention..................	truth..............	good........................
knowledge................	belief..............	success...................
courage....................	action.............	giving....................
wealth.....................	gain................	useful....................

YOUR TURN 3

Explain the following idioms.

1. To see daylight.

2. To look on the bright side.

3. You are day-dreaming.

4. To put all one's eggs in one basket.

5. Birds of a feather flock together.

6. Still waters run deep.

7. It's the last straw.

8. Discretion is better than valour.

9. Charity begins at home.
10. Better late than never.
11. To let someone down.
12. Look before you leap.
13. All that glitters is not gold.

YOUR TURN 4

Write a description of : "someone you like or admire."

....
....
....
....
....
....

A postcard from Hawaii

Part 3
Reading: Culture and Civilization

——————— British literature: The Silver Ghost ———————

She was of medium height with very small hands and feet. Her hair was ash blonde and there was very little colour in her face. Her eyes were set wide apart and were a clear pale grey. Her features were very small and regular, a straight little nose set in a small oval pale face. With such colouring, with a face that was pretty but not beautiful, she had nevertheless a quality about her that could not be denied nor ignored and that drew your eyes to her again and again. She was a little ghost, but you felt at the same time that a ghost might be possessed of more reality....

She had a singularly lovely voice; soft and clear like a small silver bell.

For some minutes she and the old lady talked of mutual friends and current events. Then Lady Tressilian said:
"Besides the pleasure of seeing you, my dear, I asked you to come because I've had rather a curious letter."

Source: From *Towards Zero*, Agatha Christie

"To all our fans, we may send you an autograph, if you're nice."

Crystel and Alex, two very famous "pop stars".

Unit 14

London taxi cabs look very different

Part 1: Conversation

A Taxi Ride

T: taxi driver   P: passenger

P : Excuse me, are you free ?

T : Sure I am. Hop in, where would you like to go ?

P : Could you take my wife and I around town for a couple of hours or so ?

T : What kind of places did you have in mind ? With just two hours, you won't have time to stop much.

P : That's all right. Well, let's visit the most famous monuments in town. After that, take us to Union Station, we have a train to catch.

T : It's up to you. Where are you from ?

P : Tokyo. How much is the fare ? Shouldn't you turn the meter on ?

T : I can if you like. Otherwise, I'd just charge you a flat rate.

P : I think I'd prefer the meter.

T : Here's the Capitol, the home of the Congress. It's free entry. And over there is the Library of Congress. It's said to be the largest in the world with over 13 million volumes.

P : My ! It does live up to its reputation.

T : That's the White House. Visits are from 10 a. m. to noon but you'll have to line up earlier.

P : Is that the Lincoln Memorial over there ?

T : Yes, it is. It's much more impressive at night.

P : We heard Washington DC is the most dangerous city in the world. How do you prevent stick-ups ?

T : You see the glass between you and me ? It's bullet-proof. When I don't like the look of my passengers, I keep it closed.

P : Say, time does fly ! We must be getting to the Station.

T : Here you are. Union Station. I hope you had a good time.

P : We certainly did. You've been a very helpful guide. How much do we owe you ?

T : The meter reads $75.

P : Here you are, $100. Keep the change for your tip.

T : Thank you very much.

P : You're welcome.

Questions

1. Write a summary of the conversation above in a few lines. (no longer than six lines)

2. Answer the following Questions.

   In Japan, how much is the fare for the taxi ? The bus ?

   Whenever you ride the train, do you use a pass ? Is it a weekly pass ?

   Which way of traveling do you prefer, the train, the taxi or the bus ? Why ?

   Have you ever ridden the bullet train ? How fast does it go ?

   How much is a one-way ticket from Tokyo to Kyoto ?

Exercises

A. Choose the correct answer.

1. What ....if Jack arrives ?
   - a. you expect to do
   - b. do you expect me
   - c. do you expect me to do
   - d. you expect me to do

2. What is the ....train station ?
   - a. most near
   - b. nearer
   - c. more near
   - d. nearest

3. There are more than five ....cabs in New York City.
   - a. thousand of
   - b. thousand
   - c. thousands
   - d. thousands of

4. My father is ....pilot.

      a. how good   b. such good   c. what   d. such a good

5. Don't forget to give Peter the invitation when you...........him.

      a. 'll see   b. see   c. will see   d. shall see

6. Send it to him yourself since you.............where he lives.

      a. know   b. knew   c. knowing   d. have known

B. Translate the following sentences.

1. This cab can't take more than five passengers.

    ....

2. The fare is shown on the meter.

    ....

3. Careful, the door isn't closed right.

    ....

4. This man is a good driver. He got us to the airport on time.

    ....

5. Is there an extra charge for the bag in the trunk ?

    ....

6. How much of a tip do you give a taxi-driver in the U.S.A ?

    ....

7. Sorry I haven't any change.

    ....

8. Can you call me a cab please ?

    ....

9. The cab will pick you up in about half an hour.

....

10. Can you take us to the Hilton Hotel ?

....

Part 2: American VS British English

US	GB
truck	lorry
cab / taxi	taxi
sidewalk	pavement
to cancel (canceled)	to cancel (cancelled)
to travel (traveled)	to travel (travelled)
program	programme
catalog	catalogue

GRAMMAR

The use of **so much** and **so many**

Examples:
- Bill Gates has got **so much** money.
- Why do you talk **so much** ?
- I have **so many** things I want to talk to you about.
- You've got **so many** cars. Are you collecting them ?

Rules: Use *so much* with the singular and *so many* with the plural.

YOUR TURN 1

Complete the following sentences with *so much* or *so many*.

1. Bob won't come to our party. He says he has ....things to do.
2. Susan, you shouldn't eat..............
3. Mr. Watson has ....pets that he can't feed them all now.
4. In my class there are ....good students.
5. I've got ....to do but I'm already so tired.
6. This diamond ring costs ....!

YOUR TURN 2

Complete the following sentences using a preposition.

1. This place looks different ....what I thought it would look like.
2. This will come in very useful...........him.
3. You are always laughing..............her.
4. I am longing ....go to England.
5. Is that a map ....England.
6. They pray ....peace in Irak every day.
7. Illness prevents him................coming.

YOUR TURN 3

Write sentences with the following words.

1. lucky: ....
2. human: ....
3. light: ....
4. sad: ....
5. happy: ....
6. prey: ....
7. pray: ....

8. rise: ....

9. raise: ....

10. lay: ....

11. lie: ....

12. discover: ....

13. invent: ....

14. remember: ....

15. remind: ....

YOUR TURN 4

Write nouns corresponding to the following verbs.

to play......................	to please......................	to fail...........................
to taste......................	to speak......................	to give..........................
to hate......................	to agree......................	to attend......................
to die......................	to rob..........................	to arrive......................
to see......................	to lose..........................	to steal..........................

Part 3
Reading: Culture and Civilization

——————The Star-Spangled Banner——————
The National Anthem of the United States of America

Oh, say can you see by the dawn's early light.
What so proudly we hailed at the twilight's last gleaming ?
Whose broad stripes and bright stars thru the perilous fight,
O'er the ramparts we watched were so gallantly streaming ?
And the rocket's red glare, the bombs bursting in air,
Gave proof through the night that our flag was still there.
Oh, say does that star-spangled banner yet wave.
O'er the land of the free and the home of the brave ?

On the shore, dimly seen through the mists of the deep,

Where the foe's haughty host in dread silence reposes,
What is that which the breeze, o'er the towering steep,
As it fitfully blows, half conceals, half discloses ?
Now it catches the gleam of the morning's first beam,
In full glory reflected now shines in the stream:
'Tis the star-spangled banner ! Oh long may it wave.
O'er the land of the free and the home of the brave !

And where is that band who so vauntingly swore.
That the havoc of war and the battle's confusion,
A home and a country should leave us no more !
Their blood has washed out their foul footsteps' pollution.
No refuge could save the hireling and slave.
From the terror of flight, or the gloom of the grave:
And the star-spangled banner in triumph doth wave.
O'er the land of the free and the home of the brave !

Oh! thus be it ever, when freemen shall stand.
Between their loved home and the war's desolation !
Blest with victory and peace, may the heav'n rescued land.
Praise the Power that hath made and preserved us a nation.
Then conquer we must, when our cause it is just,
And this be our motto: "In God is our trust."
And the star-spangled banner in triumph shall wave.
O'er the land of the free and the home of the brave !

Source: www.usembassy.hu/anthem.htm

God Save The King

The National Anthem of the United Kingdom

The first verse is usually sung on official occasions:

> God save our gracious King !
> Long live our noble King !
> God save the King !
> Send him victorious,
> Happy and glorious,
> Long to reign over us,
> God save the King.

The second verse is sung occasionally:

> Thy choicest gifts in store
> On him be pleased to pour,
> Long may he reign.
> May he defend our laws,
> And give us ever cause,
> To sing with heart and voice,
> God save the King.

Oh No ! The pharmacy is closed ! What a pity !

How old is London Tower Bridge ?

Unit 15

Is there a post office nearby ?

Part 1: Conversation

—————————————At the Post Office—————————

C: clerk   G: gentleman

C : Hello. How can I help you ?

G : I need some stamps. Can I get them at this window ?

C : Certainly. Do you want airmail or regular ?

G : Airmail please. They're for overseas, Japan.

C : How many do you want ?

G : Three for these letters and ten for these post cards.

C : Here you are. Will that be all ?

G : No. I've also got this little package going to Tokyo, Japan that I would like to send.

C : For your package, fill out these customs slips stating contents and value.

G : It's only CDs for a friend.

C : Is that everything ?

G : Yes, that's all.

C : That'll be £10.50

G : Here you are. Where can I mail these letters ?

C : You can drop them in the airmail slot over there.

G : One more thing. Could you please tell me how long it takes for a letter to reach Japan ?

C : Certainly. It takes about a week.

G : Thank you very much.

C : You're welcome.

Questions

1. Write summary of the conversation above in a few lines. (no longer than six lines)

2. Answer the following questions.

 In Japan, what is the price of a stamp for a post card ? For a regular letter ?

 Do you have friends overseas ? If yes, how often do you write to him / her / them ?

 If no, would you like to have a pen-friend ? Why ?

 How many e-mails do you receive per day ? How many do you send ?

 Which type of mail do you prefer, e-mail or hand written mail ? Why ? (give at least three reasons)

 How many New Year Cards have you received this year ? And how many did you send to your friends ?

Exercises

A. Choose the correct answer.

 1. Bob, listen. It's no use...................
   a. to complain   b. complain   c. of complaining   d. complaining

 2. I heard her ....to herself.
   a. of talking   b. to talk   c. talk   d. talked

 3. My parents like people to..................and eat at home.
   a. comes   b. come   c. who comes   d. coming

 4. We didn't know his father was ....
   a. teacher   b. as teacher c. not teacher   d. a teacher

5. She has a ....old daughter.
   a. fifteen-year-   b. fifteen year   c. fifteen year's
   d. fifteen years

6. He ....the same bike for ten years.
   a. is owning   b. has owned   c. own   d. is owned

7. Listen, someone ....at the door.
   a. knock   b. 's knocking   c. knocking   d. knocks

8. How ....time will you need ?
   a. many much   b. much more   c. many more   d. more

9. What ....could they do ?
   a. else   b. different   c. otherwise   d. other

10. We'd like John...................us the whole story.
    a. tells   b. told   c. should tell   d. to tell

B. Translate the following sentences.

1. I'd like to send this letter Special Delivery.

   ....

2. Could you help me fill out this form, please ?

   ....

3. Write the name of the addressee in block letters.

   ....

4. Can you weigh this parcel for me please ?

   ....

5. Is there any mail for me ?

   ....

6. You've forgotten the Zip codes on all your letters, Sir.

....

7. I would like to send a registered letter.

....

8. How much is an airmail letter to Japan ?

....

9. Where can I buy envelopes and post cards ?

....

10. When is the Post Office open ?

....

Part 2: American VS British English

US	GB
to mail	to post
mailbox	post box
mailman	postman
window	counter, desk
package	parcel
regular	ordinary
to fill out	fill up
ZIP code	postal code
(Zone of Improved Postage)	
General Delivery	Poste-Restante

GRAMMAR

Part 1

The use of **speak** and **talk**

Examples:

- Can you **speak** English ?
- I must **speak to** the teacher.
- I was **talking to** Jim when the phone rang.
- An old friend came over yesterday. We **talked** until late at night.

Rules: 1. Use *talk* to describe a conversational situation and *speak* for a monologue situation.

    2. Use *speak* to ask if someone knows about a language.

YOUR TURN 1

Complete the following sentences with *talk* or *speak*.

1. I'd like to be able to ....English fluently.
2. Peter and I ....for hours yesterday.
3. (On the phone) Can I ....to (with) David, please ?
4. When I heard the news, I was so shocked that I couldn't ....
5. Our English teacher caught a cold and lost his voice. Now he can't ....
6. I hope you two are not ....about me.

Part 2

The use of **hear** and **listen (to)**

Examples:

- I can't **hear** anything.
- **Listen** ! Can you **hear** the birds singing ?

Rules: *Listen* is used with the preposition **to**. ***Hear*** does not need a preposition.

YOUR TURN 2

Complete the following sentences with *hear* or *listen (to)*.

1. ....! I can ....the train.
2. This kid is so disobedient. He never..................when I talk to him.
3. I ....someone knocking at the door.
4. My brother always.................... the news in the morning.
5. Would you like to ....my new CD ?
6. Can you speak louder, please ? I can't ....anything.

YOUR TURN 3

Write the opposite of the following words.

giving............................. beauty.......................... gain...............................

permission..................... success......................... difficulty.......................

respect........................... credit........................... innocence......................

YOUR TURN 4

Explain the following idioms:

1. To commit a crime in cold blood.
2. You are day-dreaming.
3. You have put your foot in it.
4. To be out of pocket.
5. To have cold feet.
6. He has one foot in the grave.
7. To rack one's brains.
8. Her bark is worse than her bite.
9. He is the black sheep of the family.
10. His manner is off-hand.
11. It was on the tip of my tongue.

Part 3
Reading: Culture and Civilization

———————— Letters: inquiries and replies ————————

A.

2-15-1 Fujimi Chiyoda-ku
Tokyo 102-8178
Japan

January 24 2005

Dear Sir,
My wife and I would like to stay in Bethesda for one week and wondered if you could let us know your charges for the summer season. We would prefer a double bed. Please let us know what facilities you provide.
Yours sincerely,

Shoichiro Tanaka

I believe you when you say this is the biggest shopping mall in the world !

B.

SUNSET MOTEL
Surrey wood Lane
Bethesda
MD 20817
USA
January 25 2005

Dear Mr. Tanaka,
Thank you for your inquiry about our terms for the summer 2005
season. The daily charge for a double bed room would be $50 linen
included. We can offer you a reduction for stays longer than one week.
There is hot and cold running water in all bedrooms.
Yours Sincerely,
The Manager
M. Brenna

Questions

1. What is the purpose of the letter A ?
2. Who wrote the letter B ? For what purpose ?

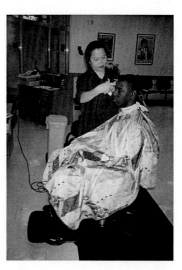

Do you know a good place
where I can go have my
hair cut ?

Job Applications

5-10-14 Kamishakujii
Nerima-ku
Tokyo 177-0042
Japan

25th January, 2005

The Staff Manager,
Jaecom Ltd,
40 Canon's Hill
Old Coulsdon,
Surrey, CR5 1HB
GB
Dear Sir or Madam,

It was with great interest that I read your advertisement in today's
Times. I would like to apply for the post of secretary in your
Telecommunications Consultancy and Project Management Department.
I speak fluent English, and French.
I enclose a copy of my curriculum vitae. Please do not hesitate to
contact me if you require any further details.

Yours faithfully,

Michiko Nakagawa

Questions

1. Who wrote the letter above ?
2. What is its purpose ?

CURRICULUM VITAE

NAME: Michiko NAKAGAWA

ADDRESS: 5-10-14 Kamishakujii
             Nerima-ku
             Tokyo 177-0042
             Japan
TELEPHONE: (81) 03 7432-2925

DATE OF BIRTH: 25. 7. 1980

MARITAL STATUS: Single

NATIONALITY: Japanese

EDUCATION: Diploma in Information Management
           Daito University Tokyo (March 2000)
           B.A in English with French,
           University of London (May 2002)
           Diploma in French Language Studies
           Alliance Francaise (June 2003)
Professional Experience:
           Trilingual Secretarial Diploma, delivered by the British
           Chamber of Commerce (August 2004)

The following have agreed to provide references:

Ms. Judith Smith, London Chamber of Commerce, SE4 3SD
Dr. Isamu Noguchi, Daito University, Tokyo 102-8178

The beauty of the nature

A breathtaking view of WAIKIKI

Appendix

I. The Fifty Stars

States	Nicknames	Capital City
Alabama (Al)	Yellowhammer State	Montgomery
Alaska (AK)	The Last Frontier	Juneau
Arizona (AZ)	Grand Canyon State	Phoenix
Arkansas (AR)	The Natural State	Little Rock
California (CA)	Golden State	Sacramento
Colorado (CO)	Centennial State	Denver
Connecticut (CT)	Constitution State	Hartford
Delaware (DE)	Diamond State	Dover
Florida (FL)	Sunshine State	Tallahassee
Georgia (GA)	Peach State	Atlanta
Hawaii (HI)	Aloha State	Honolulu
Idaho (ID)	Gem State	Boise
Illinois (Il)	Prairie State	Springfield
Indiana (IN)	Hoosier State	Indianapolis
Iowa (IA)	Hawkeye State	Des Moines
Kansas (KS)	Sunflower State	Topeka
Kentucky (KY)	Bluegrass State	Frankfort
Louisiana (LA)	Pelican State	Baton Rouge
Maine (ME)	Pine Tree State	Augusta
Maryland (MD)	Free State	Annapolis
Massachusetts (MA)	Bay State	Boston
Michigan (MI)	Wolverine State	Lansing
Minnesota (MN)	North Star State	St Paul
Mississippi (MS)	Magnolia State	Jackson
Missouri (MO)	Show-me State	Jefferson City
Montana (MT)	Treasure State	Helena
Nebraska (NE)	Cornhusker State	Lincoln
Nevada (NE)	Sagebrush State	Carson City

States	Nicknames	Capital City
New Hampshire (NH)	Granite State	Concord
New Jersey (NJ)	Garden State	Trenton
New Mexico (NM)	Land of Enchantment	Santa Fe
New York (NY)	Empire State	Albany
North Carolina (NC)	Tar Heel State	Raleigh
North Dakota (ND)	Sioux State	Bismarck
Ohio (OH)	Buckeye State	Columbus
Oklahoma (OK)	Sooner State	Oklahoma City
Oregon (OR)	Beaver State	Salem
Pennsylvania (PA)	Keystone State	Harrisburg
Rhode Island (RI)	The Ocean State	Providence
South Carolina (SC)	Palmetto State	Columbia
South Dakota (SD)	Coyote State	Pierre
Tennessee (TN)	Volunteer State	Nashville
Texas (TX)	Lone Star State	Austin
Utah (UT)	Beehive State	Salt Lake City
Vermont (VT)	Green Mountain State	Montpelier
Virginia (VA)	The Old Dominion	Richmond
Washington (WA)	Evergreen State	Olympia
West Virginia (WV)	Mountain State	Charleston
Wisconsin (WI)	Badger State	Madison
Wyoming (WY)	Equality State	Cheyenne

II. Irregular Verbs

Present	Past	Past Participle
A		
abide	abode or abided	abode or abided
arise	arose	risen
awake	awoke	awaked
B		
be	was / were	been
beat	beat	beaten
become	became	become
begin	began	begun
bend	bent	bent
bet	bet	bet
bind	bound	bound
bite	bit	bitten
bleed	bled	bled
blow	blew	blown
break	broke	broken
bring	brought	brought
build	built	built
burn	burnt	burnt
burst	burst	burst
buy	bought	bought
C		
cast	cast	cast
catch	caught	caught
choose	chose	chosen
cling	clung	clung
come	came	come
cost	cost	cost
creep	crept	crept
cut	cut	cut

Present	Past	Past Participle
D		
deal	dealt	dealt
dig	dug	dug
do	did	done
draw	drew	drown
dream	dreamt	dreamt
drink	drank	drunk
drive	drove	driven
E		
eat	ate	eaten
F		
fall	fell	fallen
feed	fed	fed
feel	felt	felt
fight	fought	fought
find	found	found
fling	flung	flung
fly	flew	flown
forbid	forbade	forbidden
forget	forgot	forgotten
forgive	forgave	forgiven
freeze	froze	frozen
G		
get	got	got / gotten (US)
give	gave	given
go	went	gone
grind	ground	ground
grow	grew	grown

Present	*Past*	*Past Participle*
H		
hang	hung	hung
have	had	had
hear	heard	heard
hide	hid	hidden
hit	hit	hit
hold	held	held
hurt	hurt	hurt
K		
keep	kept	kept
kneel	knelt	knelt
know	knew	known
L		
lay	laid	laid
lead	led	led
learn	learnt	learnt
leave	left	left
lend	lent	lent
let	let	let
lie	lay	lain
light	lit	lit
lose	lost	lost
M		
make	made	made
mean	meant	meant
meet	met	met
mow	mowed	mown or mowed
P		
pay	paid	paid
put	put	put

Present	Past	Past Participle
Q		
quit	quit or quitted	quit or quitted
R		
read	read	read
ride	rode	ridden
ring	rang	rung
rise	rose	risen
run	ran	run
S		
saw	sawed	sawed or sawn
say	said	said
see	saw	seen
seek	sought	sought
sell	sold	sold
send	sent	sent
set	set	set
sew	sewed	sewed or sewn
shake	shook	shaken
shine	shone	shone
shoot	shot	shot
show	showed	shown
shrink	shrank	shrank
shut	shut	shut
sing	sang	sung
sink	sank	sunk
sit	sat	sat
slay	slew	slain
sleep	slept	slept
slide	slid	slid
smell	smelled or smelt	smelled or smelt
smite	smote	smitten
sow	sowed	sowed or sown

Present	Past	Past Participle
speak	spoke	spoken
spell	spelt	spelt
spend	spent	spent
spill	spilt	spilt
spread	spread	spread
spring	sprang	sprung
stand	stood	stood
steal	stole	stolen
stick	stuck	stuck
sting	stung	stung
stink	stank	stunk
strike	struck	struck
swear	swore	sworn
sweep	swept	swept
swim	swam	swum
swing	swung	swung

T

take	took	taken
teach	taught	taught
tear	tore	torn
tell	told	told
think	thought	thought
thrive	throve or thrived	thriven or thrived
throw	threw	thrown
thrust	thrust	thrust
tread	trod	trodden

U

undergo	underwent	undergone
understand	understood	understood

Present	Past	Past Participle

W

Present	Past	Past Participle
wake	woke	woken
wear	wore	worn
weave	wove	woven
weep	wept	wept
win	won	won
wind	wound	wound
withdraw	withdrew	withdrawn
wring	wrung	wrung
write	wrote	written

WATCH OUT !

Present	Past	Past Participle
to feel	felt	felt
to fall	fell	fallen
to fill	filled	filled
to fly	flew	flown
to flow	flowed	flowed
to leave	left	left
to live	lived	lived
to lie	lay	lain
to lay	laid	laid
to lie	lied	lied
to think	thought	thought
to sink	sank	sunk

III. Measures and Weights

A. Linear measure

1 inch (in.) = 2.54 cm   1 foot (ft.) = 12 in. = 0.305 m

1 yard (yd.) = 3 feet = 0.915 m   1 furlong = 222 yds.

1 (stature) mile (land) = 1,760 yards = 1,609 meters

1 (nautical) mile (sea) = 1,853 m   1 knot = 1 naut. m. per hour

B. Area measure

1 square inch (sq. in.) = 6.45 sq. cm

1 square foot (sq. ft.) = 929 sq. cm

1 acre = 0.40 hectare or 4,000 sq. meters

1 square mile = 259 hectares or 2.59 sq. km

C. Cubic measure

1 cubic inch = 16.4 cc   1 cubic foot = 28316 cc

D. Capacity (US customary measures are different from British ones)

Liquids:	US	British	Solids
1 pint (pt.)	0.47 l.	0.56 l.	1 pint 0.55 liter
1 quart (qt.)	0.94 l.	1.12 l.	1 quart 1.10 liter
1 gallon (gal.)	3.785 l.	4.54 l.	1 peck 8.81 liters
			1 bushel 35.23 liters
1 barrel (bbl.) of:			or 32 pounds of oats
liquors	31 gal.	118 liters	or 48 pounds of barley
petroleum	42 gal.	159 liters	or 50 pounds of wheat
other liquids	31.5 gal.	119 liters	or 56 pounds of corn

E. Weight

1 ounce (oz.) = 28.35 grams   1 pound (lb.) = 453 gr.

1 (US) hundredweight (cwt.) = 100 lbs. = 45.36 kg

1 (British) hundredweight = (roughly) 50 kg

1 ton (gross or long) = 2,240 pounds = 1,016 kg (the same as British)

1 ton (net or short) = 2,000 pounds = 907 kg

F. To Convert

centimeters	into	inches	multiply by	0.3937
cubic cm	into	cubic in.	multiply by	0.06102
hectares	into	acres	multiply by	2.471
kilograms	into	pounds	multiply by	2.205
kilometers	into	miles	multiply by	0.6214
liters	into	cubic in.	multiply by	61.02
liters	into	pints (US liq.)	multiply by	2.113
meters	into	feet	multiply by	3.281
kg. per–sq. cm.	into	lbs. per–sq. in.	multiply by	14.22

G. Temperatures

Centigrade	Fahrenheit
0°	32°
10	50
15	59
20	68
100	212

To convert

$°C$ **into** $°F$: $× 9 ÷ 5 + 32$

$°F$ **into** $°C$: $− 32 × 5 ÷ 9$

IV. Specialized Vocabularies

A. The Parts of the Body

Head	Skull	Hair	Nape of the neck
Temples	Face	Forehead	Ears
Eyebrows	Eyelids	Eyelashes	Pupils
Cheeks	Nose	Mouth	Nostrils
Lips	Teeth	Gums	Tongue
Palate	Chin	Neck	Throat
Shoulders	Arms	Elbows	Wrists
Hands	Fingers	Thumbs	Nails
Fingers-tips	Chest	Breast	Stomach
Back	Waist	Hips	Thighs
Legs	Knees	Calves	Ankles
Foot	Toes	Toe-nails	The sole of the foot
Instep	Heel	Muscles	Bones
Limbs	Spine	Trunk	Calf

B. Animals

1. Domestic

Dog	Puppy	Cat	Kitten	Mule
Horse	Mare	Foal	Donkey	Pig
Sow	Goat	Kid	Bull	Cow
Calf	Ox	Ram	Sheep	Ewe
Lamb	Pony	Piglet	Turkey	Chicken

2. Wild

Fox	Vixen	Monkey	Tortoise	Turtle
Buffalo	Snake	Hyena	Hippopotamus	Boar
Squirrel	Hare	Rabbit	Zebra	Panther
Leopard	Panther	Reindeer	Lion	Lioness
Tiger	Tigress	Mink	Otter	Bear
Elephant	Beaver	Wolf	Cub	Duckling

C. In a Bank

to open an account · to close an account · current account
deposit account · to cash a cheque · to pay in a cheque
to write a cheque · to sign a cheque · to endorse a cheque
to cross a cheque · cheque-book · blank cheque
transfer an account · overdraft · to overdraw
savings bank · bank-manager · bank-clerk
counterfoil

D. Occupations and Professions

accountant · secretary · typist · barrister
clerk · doctor · dentist · judge
surgeon · lawyer · solicitor · magistrate
detective · soldier · artist · taxi-driver
engineer · policeman · fireman · butler
bus-conductor · barber · hairdresser · shopkeeper
conductor of an orchestra · postman · guard

E. The Weather

It is raining · bad weather · fine weather · windy
foggy · misty · cold, hot, warm · sunny
snowing · hailing · showery · pouring
freezing · thawing · frosty · thundering
hail · a storm · thunder · lightning · a dense fog

F. Illness

To have a headache · toothache · backache
stomachache · a sore throat · a bad leg or arm
to see a doctor · to send for a doctor · to examine a patient
to make out a prescription (The doctor) · to faint (to pass out)
to make up a prescription (The chemist) · to catch a cold
cough · pneumonia · small-pox · measles
rheumatism · to be hospitalized · to be convalescent
to have a tooth filled or stopped · to have a tooth out

152 Appendix

V. Summary of Verb Tenses

Simple Present

My mother **studies** English everyday.

Present Progressive or Continuous

My mother **is studying** English right now.

Simple Past

Yesterday, my mom **studied** English for two hours.

Yesterday, she **spoke** English all day with one of her American friends.

Past Progressive

Yesterday, she **was studying** English at 2 pm when the phone rang.

Past Perfect

She **had studied** English for 6 years before getting married and then having children.

Present Perfect

My mom **has studied** English before...When she was a junior high school student...

Present Perfect Progressive

My mom **has been studying** at ETOGA Eikaiwa School for 4 years now.

Future with Will

She **will** still **study** English there for two more years.

Future with Be Going to

Next year she **is going to study** English in Canada for one month in the summer holidays.

Imperative !!

Study English ! Please !

Present Conditional

If my mother **studies** English hard she can get a good job.

Past Conditional

If she **had studied** English a little more she could have gotten that wonderful job at Goooogle!

If she **could have studied** English harder she would have passed with a good grade. Unfortunately, she caught the flu just before the exams.

Well done !

《著者紹介》

Paul A. ETOGA（ポール アレクサンダー・エトガ）

KAETSU UNIVERSITY（嘉悦大学）教授

etoga@kaetsu.ac.jp

（検印省略）

2005年 5 月10日　初版発行
2010年 4 月20日　第二版発行
2023年 1 月25日　第三版発行　　　　　　　　　　略称 − ENGLISH

ENGLISH For DAILY COMMUNICATION
Featuring American VS British English

著　者	Paul A. ETOGA	
発行者	塚　田　尚　寛	

発行所　東京都文京区
　　　　春日2−13−1　　**株式会社 創 成 社**

電　話 03（3868）3867　　Ｆ Ａ Ｘ 03（5802）6802
出版話 03（3868）3857　　Ｆ Ａ Ｘ 03（5802）6801
http://www.books-sosei.com　　振　替 00150-9-191261

定価はカバーに表示してあります。

©2005, 2023 Paul A. ETOGA　　　組版：でーた工房　印刷：エーヴィス・システムズ
ISBN978-4-7944-7085-0　C3082　　製本：エーヴィス・システムズ
Printed in Japan　　　　　　　　落丁・乱丁本はお取り替えいたします。

―――――――― 創成社の本 ――――――――

ENGLISH For DAILY COMMUNICATION	Paul A. ETOGA	著	2,000円
キャリアデザイン論 ―大学生のキャリア開発について―	安武伸朗 坪井晋也	編著	1,900円
キャリア開発論 ―大学生のこれからのキャリア・リテラシー―	安武伸朗 坪井晋也	編著	1,600円
はじめての原発ガイドブック ―賛成・反対を考えるための9つの論点―	楠美順理	著	1,500円
ケースで学ぶ国連平和維持活動 ― PKOの困難と挑戦の歴史 ―	石塚勝美	著	2,100円
国連PKOと国際政治 ― 理論と実践 ―	石塚勝美	著	2,300円
入門経済学	飯田幸裕 岩田幸訓	著	1,700円
ミクロ経済学 ― 計算の極意 ―	森田龍二	著	2,500円
新・大学生が出会う法律問題 ―アルバイトから犯罪・事故まで役立つ基礎知識―	信州大学経法学部	編	2,000円
大学生が出会う経済・経営問題 ―お金の話から就職活動まで役立つ基礎知識―	信州大学経済学部 経済学科	編	1,600円
これだけはおさえたい！ 保育者のための「子どもの保健」	鈴木美枝子	編著	2,200円
これだけはおさえたい！ 保育者のための「子どもの健康と安全」	鈴木美枝子	編著	2,500円
予習・復習にも役立つ社会的養護Ⅱ	松本なるみ 中安恆太 尾崎眞三	編著	2,000円
よくわかる幼稚園実習	百瀬ユカリ	著	1,800円
よくわかる保育所実習	百瀬ユカリ	著	1,700円
実習に役立つ保育技術	百瀬ユカリ	著	1,700円

(本体価格)

―――――――― 創成社 ――――――――